CAMBRIDGE LIBRARY COLLECTION

Books of enduring scholarly value

Women's Writing

The later twentieth century saw a huge wave of academic interest in women's writing, which led to the rediscovery of neglected works from a wide range of genres, periods and languages. Many books that were immensely popular and influential in their own day are now studied again, both for their own sake and for what they reveal about the social, political and cultural conditions of their time. A pioneering resource in this area is Orlando: Women's Writing in the British Isles from the Beginnings to the Present (http://orlando.cambridge.org), which provides entries on authors' lives and writing careers, contextual material, timelines, sets of internal links, and bibliographies. Its editors have made a major contribution to the selection of the works reissued in this series within the Cambridge Library Collection, which focuses on non-fiction publications by women on a wide range of subjects from astronomy to biography, music to political economy, and education to prison reform.

A Vindication of the Rights of Men

Mary Wollstonecraft (1759–1797) published *A Vindication of the Rights of Men* anonymously in 1790. The pamphlet sold out within three weeks to great acclaim; though later editions published under her own name met with notable opprobrium. It was the first of many printed responses to Edmund Burke's conservative attacks on the French Revolution, *Reflections on the Revolution in France* (1790), and it marked Wollstonecraft's entry into the adversarial public intellectual arena of the late eighteenth century. Wollstonecraft's defence of the principles of the Revolution remain rhetorically powerful. She attacked hereditary privilege and political conservatism, arguing for codified civil rights and political liberty. She also highlighted Burke's gendered language and criticised his silence on the plight of women. Wollstonecraft has inspired reverence and revulsion alike, for both her work and her lifestyle. Her prescience and nonconformity, however, have secured her position in the canon of distinguished eighteenth-century political thinkers. For more information on this author, see http://orlando. cambridge.org/public/svPeople?person_id=wollma

T0371453

Cambridge University Press has long been a pioneer in the reissuing of out-of-print titles from its own backlist, producing digital reprints of books that are still sought after by scholars and students but could not be reprinted economically using traditional technology. The Cambridge Library Collection extends this activity to a wider range of books which are still of importance to researchers and professionals, either for the source material they contain, or as landmarks in the history of their academic discipline.

Drawing from the world-renowned collections in the Cambridge University Library, and guided by the advice of experts in each subject area, Cambridge University Press is using state-of-the-art scanning machines in its own Printing House to capture the content of each book selected for inclusion. The files are processed to give a consistently clear, crisp image, and the books finished to the high quality standard for which the Press is recognised around the world. The latest print-on-demand technology ensures that the books will remain available indefinitely, and that orders for single or multiple copies can quickly be supplied.

The Cambridge Library Collection will bring back to life books of enduring scholarly value (including out-of-copyright works originally issued by other publishers) across a wide range of disciplines in the humanities and social sciences and in science and technology.

A Vindication of the Rights of Men

In a Letter to the Right Honourable Edmund Burke; Occasioned by his Reflections on the Revolution in France

M ARY W OLLSTONECRAFT

CAMBRIDGE UNIVERSITY PRESS

Cambridge, New York, Melbourne, Madrid, Cape Town, Singapore,
São Paolo, Delhi, Dubai, Tokyo

Published in the United States of America by Cambridge University Press, New York

www.cambridge.org
Information on this title: www.cambridge.org/9781108018845

© in this compilation Cambridge University Press 2010

This edition first published 1790
This digitally printed version 2010

ISBN 978-1-108-01884-5 Paperback

A

VINDICATION

OF THE

RIGHTS OF MEN,

IN A

LETTER

TO THE RIGHT HONOURABLE

EDMUND BURKE;

OCCASIONED BY

HIS REFLECTIONS

ON THE

REVOLUTION IN FRANCE.

LONDON:

PRINTED FOR J. JOHNSON,
NO. 72, ST. PAUL'S CHURCH-YARD.

M. DCC. XC

ADVERTISEMENT.

Mr. Burke's Reflections on the
French Revolution first engaged my
attention as the transient topic of the
day; and reading it more for amuse-
ment than information, my indignation was roused by the sophistical
arguments, that every moment crossed
me, in the questionable shape of natural feelings and common sense.
Many pages of the following letter were the effusions of the moment; but, swelling imperceptibly to
a considerable size, the idea was sug-
gested of publishing a short vindication

tion of *the Rights of Men.* But not having leifure or patience to follow this defultory writer through all the devious tracks in which his fancy ftarted frefh game, I have confined my ftrictures, in a great meafure, to the grand principles at which he has levelled many ingenious arguments in a very fpecious garb.

A

L E T T E R

TO THE

Right Honourable EDMUND BURKE.

––––––––––

S I R,

IT is not neceſſary, with courtly inſincerity, to apologiſe to you for thus intruding on your precious time, nor to profeſs that I think it an honour to diſcuſs an important ſubject with a man whoſe literary abilities have raiſed him to notice in the ſtate. I have not yet learned to twiſt my periods, nor, in the equivocal idiom of politeneſs, to diſguiſe my ſentiments, and imply what I ſhould be afraid to utter:

B   if,

if, therefore, in the courfe of this epiftle, I chance to exprefs contempt, and even indignation, with fome emphafis, I befeech you to believe that it is not a flight of fancy; for truth, in morals, has ever appeared to me the effence of the fublime; and, in tafte, fimplicity, the only criterion of the beautiful. But I war not with an individual when I contend for the *rights of men* and the liberty of reafon.

You fee I do not condefcend to cull my words to avoid the invidious phrafe, nor fhall I be prevented from giving a manly definition of it, by the flimfy ridicule which a lively fancy has interwoven with the prefent acceptation of the term. Reverencing the rights of humanity, I fhall dare to affert them, not intimidated by the laugh which you have raifed, or waiting till time has wiped away the tears of compaffion that you have elaborately laboured to excite.

From

From the many juft fentiments interfperfed through the letter before me, and from the whole tendency of it, I believe you to be, though a vain, yet a good man; and for this weaknefs a knowledge of human nature enables me to difcover fuch extenuating circumftances, in the very texture of your mind, that I am ready to call it amiable, and feparate the public from the private character.

I know that a lively imagination renders a man particularly calculated to fhine in converfation and thefe kind of defultory productions; and the inftantaneous applaufe which his eloquence extorts is at once a reward and a fpur. Once a wit and always a wit, is an aphorifm that has received the fanction of experience; but the man who with fcrupulous anxiety endeavours to fupport that character, can never nourifh by reflection any profound, or, if you pleafe, metaphyfical paffion. Ambition becomes only the tool of vanity, and

Reafon,

Reafon, the weather-cock of unreftrained feelings, is employed to varnifh over the faults which fhe ought to have corrected.

Sacred, however, would the infirmities and errors of a good man be, in my eyes, if they were only difplayed in a private circle; if the venial fault only rendered the wit anxious, like a celebrated beauty, to raife admiration on every occafion, and excite emotion, inftead of the calm reciprocation of mutual efteem and unimpaffioned refpect. Such vanity enlivens focial intercourfe, and forces the little great man to be always on his guard to fecure his throne; and an ingenious man, who is ever on the watch for conqueft, will, in his eagernefs to exhibit his whole ftore of knowledge, furnifh an attentive obferver with fome ufeful information, calcined by fancy and formed by tafte.

And though fome dry reafoner might whifper that the arguments were fuperficial, and

fhould

fhould even add, that the feelings which are thus oftentatioufly difplayed are often the cold declamation of the head, and not the effufions of the heart—what will thefe fhrewd remarks avail, when the witty arguments and orna-mental feelings are on a level with the com-prehenfion of the fafhionable world, and a book is found very amufing? Even the La-dies, Sir, may repeat your fprightly fallies, and retail in theatrical attitudes many of your pathetic exclamations. Senfibility is the *manie* of the day, and compaffion the virtue which is to cover a multitude of vices, whilft juftice is left to mourn in fullen filence, and balance truth in vain.

In life, an honeft man with a confined un-derftanding, is frequently the flave of his habits and the dupe of his feelings, whilft the man with a clearer head and colder heart makes the paffions of others bend to his intereft; but truly fublime is that character who acts from

principle,

principle, and governs the inferior springs of activity without slackening their vigour, whose feelings give vital heat to his resolves, but never hurry him into feverish eccentricities.

However, as you have informed us that respect chills love, it is natural to conclude, that all your pretty flights arise from your pampered sensibility; and that, vain of this fancied pre-eminence of organs, you foster every emotion till the inmes, mounting to your brain, dispel the sober suggestions of reason. It is not in this view surprising, that when you should argue you become impassioned, and that reflection inflames your imagination, instead of enlightening your understanding.

Quitting now the flowers of rhetoric, let us, Sir, reason together; and, believe me, I should not have meddled with these troubled waters, in order to point out your inconsistencies, if your wit had not burnished up some rusty

baneful

(7)

baneful opinions, and fwelled the fhallow current of ridicule till it refembled the flow of reafon, and prefumed to be the teſt of truth.

I fhall not attempt to follow you through " horfe-way and foot-path;" but, attacking the foundation of your opinions, I fhall leave the fuperftructure to find a centre of gravity on which it may lean till fome ftrong blaſt puffs it into air; or your teeming fancy, which the ripening judgment of fixty years has not tamed, produces another Chinefe erection, to ftare, at every turn, the plain country people in the face, who bluntly call fuch an airy edifice—a folly.

The birthright of man, to give you, Sir, a fhort definition of this difputed right, is fuch a degree of liberty, civil and religious, as is compatible with the liberty of the other individuals whom he is united with in a focial compact.

B 4   Liberty,

Liberty, in this simple, unsophisticated sense, I acknowledge, is a fair idea that has never yet received a form in the various governments that have been established on our beauteous globe; the demon of property has ever been at hand to encroach on the sacred rights of men; but that it results from the eternal foundation of right—from immutable truth—who will presume to deny, that pretends to rationality—if reason has led them to build their morality [a] and religion on an everlasting foundation—the attributes of God?

I glow with indignation when I attempt, methodically, to unravel your slavish paradoxes, in which I can find no fixed first principle to refute; I shall not, therefore, conde-

[a] As religion is included in my idea of morality, I should not have mentioned the term without specifying all the simple ideas which that comprehensive word generalizes; but as the charge of atheism has been very freely banded about in the letter I am considering, I condescend to guard against misrepresentation.

fcend

(9)

fcend to fhew where you affirm in one page what
you deny in another; and how frequently you
draw conclufions without any previous pre-
mifes:—it would be fomething like cowardice
to fight with a man who had never excercifed
the weapons which his opponent chofe to
combat with.

I know that you have a mortal antipathy
to reafon ; but, if there is any thing like argument, or firft principles, in your wild declamation, behold the refult:—that we are to reverence the ruft of antiquity, and term the
unnatural cuftoms, which ignorance and miftaken felf-intereft have confolidated, the fage
fruit of experience: and that, if we do difcover fome errors, our *feelings* fhould lead
us to excufe, with blind love, or unprincipled
filial affection, the venerable veftiges of ancient days. Thefe are gothic notions of
beauty—the ivy is beautiful though it infi-
dioufly

dioufly deftroys the trunk from which it receives fupport.

Further, that we ought cautioufly to remain for ever in frozen inactivity, becaufe a thaw that nourifhes the foil fpreads a temporary inundation; and that the fear of rifking any thing fhould prevent a ftruggle for the moft eftimable advantages. This is found reafoning, I grant, in the mouth of the rich and fhort-fighted.

Yes, Sir, the ftrong gained riches, the few have facrificed the many to their vices; and, to be able to pamper their appetites, and fupinely exift without exercifing mind or body, they have ceafed to be men.—They, indeed, would deferve compaffion, if injuftice was not foftened by the tyrant's plea—neceffity; if prefcription was not raifed as an immortal boundary againft innovation. Their minds, in fact, inftead of being cultivated, have been

fo

fo warped by education, that it may require fome ages to bring them back to nature, and enable them to fee their true intereft.

The civilization which has taken place in Europe has been very partial, and, like every cuftom that an arbitrary point of honour has eftablifhed, refines the manners at the expence of morals.—And what has ftopped it ?— hereditary property—hereditary honours. The man has been changed into an artificial monfter by the ftation in which he was born, and the confequent homage that benumbed his faculties like the torpedo's touch,—or a being, with a capacity of reafoning, would have difcovered, as his faculties unfolded, that true happinefs arofe from the friendfhip and intimacy which can only be enjoyed by equals ; and that charity is not a condefcending diftribution of alms, but an intercourfe of good offices and mutual benefits, founded on refpect for humanity.

The

The poor wretch, whofe *inelegant* diftrefs
has extorted from a mixed feeling of difguft
and animal fympathy prefent relief, would
have been confidered as a man, whofe mifery
demanded a part of his birthright, fuppofing
him to be induftrious; but fhould his vices
have reduced him to poverty, he muft then
have addreffed his fellow-men as weak beings,
fubject to like paffions, who ought to forgive,
becaufe they expect to be forgiven, for fuffering the impulfe of the moment to filence the
fuggeftions of confcience, or reafon, which
you will; for, in my view of things, they are
fynonymous terms.

Will Mr. Burke be at the trouble to inform
us, how far we are to go back to difcover the
rights of men, fince the light of reafon is
fuch a fallacious guide that none but fools
truft to its cold inveftigation?

In the infancy of fociety, confining our
view to our own country, cuftoms were efta-
bliſhed

blifhed by the lawlefs power of an ambitious individual, or a weak prince was obilged to comply with every demand of the licentious barbarous infurgents, who difputed his autho- rity with irrefragable arguments at the point of their fwords, or the more fpecious requefts of the Parliament, who only allowed him con- ditional fupplies.

Are thefe the venerable pillars of our confti- tution? And is Magna Charta to reft for its chief fupport on a former grant, which reverts to another, till chaos becomes the bafe of the mighty ftructure—or we cannot tell what?— for coherence, without fome pervading princi- ple of order, is a folecifm.

Speaking of Edward the IIId. Hume ob- ferves, that ' he was a prince of great capacity, ' not governed by favourites, not led aftray by ' any unruly paffion, fenfible that nothing could ' be more effential to his interefts than to keep ' on good terms with his people: yet, on the

7   ' whole,

' whole, it appears that government, at beft,
' was only a barbarous monarchy, not regu-
' lated by any fixed maxims, or bounded by
' any certain or undifputed rights, which in
' practice were regularly obferved. The king
' conducted himfelf by one fet of principles;
' the Barons by another; the Commons by a
' third; the Clergy by a fourth. All thefe
' fyftems of government were oppofite and
' incompatible: each of them prevailed in its
' turn, as incidents were favourable to it:
' a great prince rendered the monarchal
' power predominant: the weaknefs of a king
' gave reins to the ariftocracy: a fuperftitious
' age faw the clergy triumphant: the people,
' for whom chiefly government was inftituted,
' and who chiefly deferve confideration, were
' the weakeft of the whole.'

And juft before that aufpicious æra, the
fourteenth century, during the reign of that
weak prince, Richard II. whofe total inca-
pacity

pacity to manage the reins of power, and
keep in fubjection his haughty Barons, rendered him a mere cypher, the Houfe of
Commons, to whom he was obliged frequently to apply, not only for fubfidies, but affiftance to quell infurrections that the contempt
in which he was held naturally gave rife to,
gradually rofe into power; for whenever they
granted fupplies to the King, they demanded
in return, though it bore the name of petition,
a confirmation, or the renewal of former char-
ters, which had been infringed, and even
utterly difregarded by the King and his fedi-
tious Barons, who principally held their independence of the crown by force of arms,
and the encouragement which they gave to
robbers and villains, who infefted the country,
and lived by rapine and violence.

To what dreadful extremities were the
poorer fort reduced, their property, the fruit
of their induftry, being entirely at the dif-
pofal

pofal of their lords, who were fo many petty tyrants !

In return for the fupplies and affiftance which the king received from the commons, they demanded privileges, which Edward, in his diftrefs for money to profecute the numerous wars in which he was engaged during the greateft part of his reign, was conftrained to grant them; fo that by degrees they rofe to power, and became a check on both king and nobles. Thus was the foundation of our liberty eftablifhed, chiefly through the wants of the king, who was more intent on being fupplied for the moment, in order to carry on his wars and ambitious projects, than aware of the blow he was giving to kingly power in raifing a body of men, who in the end might oppofe tyranny and oppreffion, and effectually guard the fubject's property from feizure and confifcation;—Richard's weaknefs completed what Edward's ambition began.

At

At this period, it is true, Wickliffe opened a vifta for reafon by attacking fome of the moft pernicious tenets of the church of Rome —ftill where was the dignity of thinking of the fourteenth century?

A Roman Catholic, it is true, enlightened by the reformation, might, with fingular propriety, celebrate the epocha that preceded it, to turn our thoughts from former enormities; but a Proteftant muft acknowledge that this faint dawn of liberty only made the fubfiding darknefs more vifible; and that the boafted virtues of that century all bear the ftamp of ftupid pride and headftrong barbarifm. Then civility was called condefcenfion, and oftentatious charity humanity; and men were content to borrow their virtues, or, to fpeak with more propriety, their confequence, from pofterity, rather than undertake the arduous tafk of acquiring it for themfelves.

C   The

The imperfection of all modern governments muft, without waiting to repeat the
trite remark, that all human inftitutions are
unavoidably imperfect, in a great meafure have
arifen from this fimple circumftance, that the
conftitution, if fuch an heterogeneous mafs
deferve that name, was fettled in the dark
days of ignorance, when the minds of men
were fhackled by the groffeft prejudices and
moft immoral fuperftition. And does this
fagacious philofopher recommend night as the
fitteft time to analyze a ray of light?

Are we to feek for the rights of men in the
ages when a few marks were the only penalty
impofed for the life of a man, and death for
death when the property of the rich was
touched? when—I blufh to difcover the depra-
vity of our nature—when a deer was killed!
Are thefe the laws that it is natural to love,
and facrilegious to invade?—Were the rights
of

of men underftood when the law authorifed or tolerated murder?—or is power and right the fame?

In truth, all your declamation leads to this conclufion; and, when you call yourfelf a friend of liberty, afk your own heart whether it would not be more confiftent to ftyle your-felf the champion of property, the adorer of the golden image which power has fet up?— And, when you are examining your heart, if it would not be too much like mathematical drudgery, to which a fine imagination very re-luctantly ftoops, enquire further, how it is con-fiftent with the vulgar notions of honefty, and the foundation of morality—truth; for a man to boaft of his virtue and independence, when he cannot forget that he is at the moment en-joying the wages of falfehood [b]; and that, in a fkulking, unmanly way, he has fecured him-

[b] See Mr. Burke's Bills for œconomical reform.

felf

felf a penfion of fifteen hundred pounds per annum on the Irifh eftablifhment ?

Do honeft men, Sir, for I am not rifing to the refined principle of honour, ever receive the reward of their public fervices, or fecret affiftance, in the name of *another* ?

But to return from a degreffion which you will more perfectly underftand than any of my readers—on what principle you, Sir, can juftify the reformation, which tore up by the roots an old eftablifhment, I cannot guefs— but, I beg your pardon, perhaps you do not wifh to juftify it—and have fome mental refervation to excufe you, to yourfelf, for not openly avowing your reverence. Or, to go further back;—had you been a Jew—you muft have joined in the cry, crucify him !— crucify him ! The promulgator of a new doc- trine, and the violator of old laws and cuftoms, that did not, like ours, melt into darknefs and

ignorance,

ignorance, but, refted on Divine authority, muft have been a dangerous innovator, in your eyes, particularly if you had not been informed that the Carpenter's Son was of the ftock and lineage of David. But there is no end to the arguments which might be deduced to combat fuch palpable abfurdities, by fhewing the in-confiftencies which are involved in a direful train of falfe opinions.

Is it neceffary to repeat, that there are rights which we received, at our birth, as men, when we were raifed above the brute creation by the power of improving ourfelves—and that we receive thefe not from our forefathers, but from God?

My father may diffipate his property, yet I have no right to complain;—but if he fhould attempt to fell me for a flave, or fetter me with laws contrary to reafon; nature, in enabling me to difcern good from evil, teaches me to break the ignoble chain, and not to

believe

believe that bread becomes flesh, and wine blood, becaufe my parents fwallowed the Euchariſt with this blind perſuaſion.

There is no end to this fubmiſſion to authority—fome where it muſt ſtop, or we return to barbarifm; and the capacity of improvement is a cheat, an ignis-fatuus, that leads us from the inviting meadow into bogs and dunghills. If it be allowed that many of the precautions, with which any alteration was made, in our government, were prudent, it rather proves its weaknefs than fubſtantiates an opinion of the foundnefs of the ſtamina, or the excellence of the conſtitution.

But on what principle Mr. Burke could defend American independence, I cannot conceive; for the whole tenor of his plauſible arguments fettles flavery on an everlaſting foundation. Allowing his fervile reverence for antiquity, and prudent attention to ſelf-intereſt, to have the force which he infiſts on,

it

it ought never to be aboliſhed; and, becauſe our
ignorant forefathers, not underſtanding the
native dignity of man, ſanctioned a traffic that
outrages every ſuggeſtion of reaſon and religion,
we are to ſubmit to the inhuman cuſtom, and
term an atrocious inſult to humanity the love of
our country and a proper ſubmiſſio to thoſe
laws which ſecure our property.— Security of
property! Behold, in a few words, the definition of Engliſh liberty. And to this ſelfiſh
principle every nobler one is ſacrificed.—The
Briton takes place of the man, and the image
of God is loſt in the citizen! But it is not that
enthuſiaſtic flame which in Greece and Rome
conſumed every ſordid paſſion: no, ſelf is
the focus; and the diſparting rays riſe not
above our foggy atmoſphere. But ſoftly—it is
only the property of the rich that is ſecure;
the man who lives by the ſweat of his brow
has no aſylum from oppreſſion; the ſtrong
man may enter—when was the caſtle of the

poor

poor facred? and the bafe informer fteal him from the family that depend on his induftry for fubfiftence.

Fully fenfible of the baneful confequences that muft follow this notorious infringement on the deareft rights of men, and that it is an infernal blot on the very face of our immaculate conftitution, I cannot avoid expreffing my furprife that when you recommended our form of government as a model, you did not caution the French againft the arbitrary cuftom of preffing men for the fea fervice. You fhould have hinted to them, that property in England is much more fecure than liberty, and not have concealed that the liberty of an honeft mechanic—his all—is often facrificed to fecure the property of the rich. For it is a farce to pretend that a man fights *for his country, his hearth, or his altars,* when he has neither liberty nor property.—His property is in his nervous arms—and they are compelled to pull

a ftrange

a ftrange rope at the furly command of a tyrannic boy, who probably obtained his rank on
account of his family conne&ions, or the
proftituted vote of his father, whofe intereft
in a borough, or voice as a fenator, was very
acceptable to the minifter.

Our penal laws punifh with death the thief
who fteals a few pounds; but to take by violence, or trepan, a man, is no fuch heinous
offence.—For who fhall dare to complain of
the venerable veftige of the law that rendered
the life of a deer more facred than that of a
man ? But it was the poor man with only his
native dignity who was thus oppreffed—and
only metaphyfical fophifts and cold mathema-
ticians can difcern this infubftantial form, it is
a work of abftraction—and a *gentleman* of
lively imagination muft borrow fome drapery
from fancy before he can love or pity a man.—
Mifery, to reach your heart, I perceive, muft
have its cap and bells; your tears are referved,

very

very *naturally* considering your character, for the declamation of the theatre, or for the downfall of queens, whose rank throws a graceful veil over vices that degrade humanity; but the distress of many industrious mothers, whose *helpmates* have been torn from them, and the hungry cry of helpless babes, were vulgar sorrows that could not move your commiseration, though they might extort an alms. ' The ' tears that are shed for fictitious sorrow are ' admirably adapted,' says Rousseau, ' to make ' us proud of all the virtues which we do not ' possess.'

The baneful effects of this despotic practice we shall, in all probability, soon feel; for a number of men, who have been taken from their daily employments, will shortly be let loose on society, now the apprehension of a war no longer requires warlike preparations.

The vulgar, and by this epithet I mean not only to describe a class of people, who, working

ing

ing to fupport the body, have not had time to
cultivate their minds; but likewife thofe who,
born in the lap of affluence, have never had
their invention fharpened by neceffity, are nine
out of ten the creatures of habit and impulfe.

If I were not afraid to derange your nervous
fyftem by the bare mention of a metaphyfical
enquiry, I fhould obferve, Sir, that felf-pre-
fervation is, literally fpeaking, the firft law of
nature; and that the care neceffary to fupport
and guard the body is the firft ftep to unfold
the mind, and infpire a manly fpirit of independence. The mewing babe in fwaddling-
clothes, who is treated like a fuperior being,
may become a gentleman; but nature muft
have given him uncommon faculties if, when
pleafure hangs on every bough, he has fufficient
fortitude either to exercife his mind or body
in order to acquire perfonal merit. The paffions
are neceffary auxiliaries of reafon: a prefent
impulfe pufhes us forward, and when we dif-

cover

cover that the game did not deferve the chace,
we find that we have gone over much ground,
and not only gained many new ideas, but a
habit of thinking. The exercife of our faculties is the only folid advantage, but not the
goal we had in view when we ftarted with
fuch eagernefs.

It would be ftraying ftill further into meta-
phyfics to add, that this is one of the ftrongeft
arguments for the natural immortality of the
foul.—Every thing looks like a means, nothing
like an end, or point of reft, when we can fay,
now let us fit down and enjoy the prefent moment; our faculties and wifhes are proportioned
to the prefent fcene; we may return without
repining to our fifter clod. And, if no confcious
dignity whifpers that we are capable of relifh-
ing more refined pleafures, the thirft of truth is
allayed; and thought, the faint type of an im-
material energy, no longer bounding it knows
not where, is confined to the tenement that

affords

affords it fufficient variety.—The rich man
may then thank his God that he is not like
other men—but when is retribution to be made
to the miferable, who cry day and night for
help, and there is no one at hand to help them?
Not only mifery but immorality proceeds
from this ftretch of arbitrary authority. The
vulgar have not the power of emptying their
mind of the only ideas they imbibed whilft
their hands were employed; they cannot
quickly turn from one kind of life to another.
Preffing them entirely unhinges them; they
acquire new habits, and cannot return to their
old occupations with their former readinefs;
confequently they fall into idlenefs, drunken-
nefs, and the whole train of vices which you
ftigmatife as grofs.

The government that acts in this manner
cannot be called a good parent, nor infpire
natural (habitual is the proper word) affection,

in

in the breasts of children who are thus disregarded.

The game laws are almost as oppressive to the peasantry as press-warrants to the mechanic. In this land of liberty what is to secure the property of the poor farmer when his noble landlord chooses to plant a decoy field near his little property? The game devours the fruit of his labour; but fines and imprisonment await him if he dare to kill them—or lift up his hand to interrupt the pleasure of his lord. How many families have been plunged, in the *sporting* countries, into misery and vice by some paltry transgression of these coercive laws, by the natural consequence of that anger which a man feels when he sees the reward of his industry laid waste by unfeeling luxury?— when his children's bread is given to dogs!

You have shewn, Sir, by your silence on these heads, that your respect for rank has
swallowed

fwallowed up the common feelings of humanity; you feem to confider the poor as only the
live ftock of an eftate, the feather of hereditary
nobility. When you had fo little refpect for
the filent majefty of mifery, I am not furprifed
at your manner of treating an individual
whofe brow a mitre will never grace, and
whofe popularity may have wounded your vanity—for vanity is very fore. Even in France,
Sir, before the revolution, literary celebrity
procured a man the treatment of a gentleman;
but you are going back for your credentials of
politenefs to more diftant times,—Gothic affabi-
lity is the mode you think proper to adopt,
the condefcenfion of a Baron, not the civility
of a liberal man. Politenefs is, indeed, the
only fubftitute for humanity; or what diftin-
guifhes the civilifed man from the unlettered
favage? and he who is not governed by reafon fhould have a rule by which to fquare his
6   behaviour.

behaviour. But by what rule yeur attack on
Dr. Price's was regulated we have yet to learn.

I agree with you, Sir, that the pulpit is not
the place for political difcuffions, though it
might be more excufable to enter on fuch a
fubject, when the day was fet apart merely to
commemorate a political revolution, and no
ftated duty was encroached on. I will, however, wave this point, and allow that Dr. Price's
zeal may have carried him further than found
reafon can juftify. I do alfo moft cordially
coincide with you, that till we can fee the
remote confequences of things prefent, calamities muft appear in the ugly form of evil, and
excite our commiferation. The good educing
from them may be hid from mortal eye, or
dimly feen; whilft fympathy compels man to
feel for man, and almoft reftrains the hand
that would amputate a limb to fave the whole
body. But after making this conceffion, allow
me to ,expoftulate with you, and calmly hold

7   up

up the glafs which will fhew you your partial
feelings.

In reprobating Dr. Price's opinions you
might have fpared the man; and if you had
had but half as much reverence for the grey
hairs of virtue as for the accidental diftinctions
of rank, you would not have treated with
fuch indecent familiarity and fupercilious contempt, a member of the community whofe
talents and modeft virtues place him high
in the fcale of moral excellence. I am not
accuftomed to look up with vulgar awe, even
when mental fuperiority exalts a man above his
fellows; but ftill the fight of a man whofe habits
are fixed by piety and reafon, and virtues confolidated into goodnefs, commands my homage
—and I fhould touch his errors with a tender
hand when I made a parade of my fenfibility.
Granting, for a moment, that Dr. Price's political opinions are Utopian reveries, and that the
world is not yet fufficiently civilized to adopt

D   fuch

fuch a fublime fyftem of morality; they could, however, only be the reveries of a benevolent mind. Tottering on the verge of the grave, that worthy man in his whole life never dreamt of ftruggling for power or riches; and, if a glimpfe of the glad dawn of liberty rekindled the fire of youth in his veins, you, who could not ftand the fafcinating glance of a *great* Lady's eyes, when neither virtue nor fenfe beamed in them, might pardon his unfeemly tranfport,—if fuch it muft be deemed.

I could almoft fancy that I now fee the refpectable old man, in his pulpit, with hands clafped, and eyes devoutly fixed, praying with all the fimple energy of unaffected piety; or, when more erect, inculcating the dignity of virtue, and enforcing the doctrines his life adorns; benevolence animated each feature, and perfuafion attuned his accents; the preacher grew eloquent, who only laboured to be clear; and the refpect that he extorted, feemed only

the

the refpeÄ due to perfonified virtue and
matured wifdom.——Is this the man you
brand with fo many opprobrious epithets? he
whofe private life will ftand the teft of the
ftriÄeft enquiry—away with fuch unmanly
farcafms, and puerile conceits.—But, before I
elofe this part of my animadverfions, I muft
conviÄ you of wilful mifreprefentation, and
wanton abufe.

The doÄor, when he reafons on the neceffity of men attending fome place of public
worfhip, concifely obviates an objeÄion that
has been made in-the form of an apology,
by advifing thofe, who do not approve of our
Liturgy, and cannot find any mode of worfhip
out of the church, in which they can con-
fcientioufly join, to eftablifh one for themfelves.
This plain advice you have tortured into a
very different meaning, and reprefented the
preacher as aÄuated by a diffenting phrenfy,
recommending diffenfions, not to diffufe truth,

but

but to fpread contradictions. A fimple queftion will filence this impertinent declamation.—What is truth? A few fundamental
truths meet the firft enquiry of reafon, and
appear as clear to an unwarped mind, as that
air and bread are neceffary to enable the body
to fulfil its vital functions; but the opinions
which men difcufs with fo much heat muft be
fimplified and brought back to firft principles;
or who can difcriminate the vagaries of
the imagination, or fcrupulofity of weaknefs,
from the verdict of reafon? Let all thefe
points be demonftrated and not determined by
arbitrary authority and dark traditions; for probably, in ceafing to enquire, our reafon might
remain dormant, and delivered up, without a
curb to every impulfe of paffion, we might foon
lofe fight of the clear light which the exercife
of our underftanding no longer kept alive.
We fhould beware of confining all moral excellence to one channel, however capacious;

or,

or, if we are fo narrow-minded, we fhould not forget how much we owe to chance that our inheritance was not Mahometifm ; and that the iron hand of deftiny, in the fhape of deeply rooted authority, has not fufpended the fword of deftruction over our heads. But to return to the mifreprefentations.

ᶜ Blackftone, to whom Mr. Burke pays great deference, feems to agree with Dr. Price,

ᶜ ‘ The doctrine of *hereditary* right does by no means
‘ imply an *indefefible* right to the throne. No man will,
‘ I think, affert this, that has confidered our laws, confti-
‘ tution, and hiftory, without prejudice, and with any de-
‘ gree of attention. It is unqueftionably in the breaft of
‘ the fupreme legiflative authority of this kingdom, the
‘ King and both Houfes of Parliament, to defeat this he-
‘ reditary right; and, by particular entails, limitations,
‘ and provifions, to exclude the immediate heir, and veft
‘ the inheritance in any one elfe. This is ftrictly confo-
‘ nant to our laws and conftitution; as may be gathered
‘ from the expreffion fo frequently ufed in our ftatute
‘ books, of “ the King’s Majefty, his heirs, and fuccef-
“ fors.” In which we may obferve that, as the word
“ heirs” neceffarily implies an inheritance, or hereditary

‘ right,

Price, that the fucceffion of the King of
Great Britain depends on the choice of the
people, or that they have a power to cut it
off; but this power, as you have fully proved,
has been cautioufly exerted, and might with
more propriety be termed a *right*, than a power.
Be it fo!—but when you elaborately cited
precedents to fhew that our forefathers paid
great refpect to hereditary claims, you might
have gone back to your favourite epocha,
and fhewn their refpect for a church that ful-
minating laws have fince loaded with oppro-

' right, generally fubfifting in " the royal perfon;" fo the
' word fucceffors, diftinctly taken, muft imply that this
' inheritance may fometimes be broken through; or, that
' there may be a fucceffor, without being the heir of the
' king.'

I fhall not, however, reft in fomething like a fubter-
fuge, and quote, as partially as you have done, from
Ariftotle. Blackftone has fo cautioufly fenced round his
opinion with provifos, that it is obvious he thought
the letter of the law leaned towards your fide of the
queftion—but a blind refpect for the law is not a part of
my creed.

brium.

brium. The preponderance of inconfiftencies, when weighed with precedents, fhould leffen the moft bigotted veneration for antiquity, and force men of the eighteenth century to acknowledge, that our *canonized forefathers* were unable, or afraid, to revert to reafon, without refting on the crutch of authority; and fhould not be brought as a proof that their children are never to be allowed to walk alone.

When we doubt the infallible wifdom of our anceftors, it is only advancing on the fame ground to doubt the fincerity of the law, and the propriety of that fervile appellation—our SOVEREIGN LORD THE KING. Who were the dictators of this adulatory language of the law? Were they not courtly parafites and worldly priefts? Befides, whoever at divine fervice, whofe feelings were not deadened by habit, or their underftandings quiefcent, ever repeated without horror the fame epithets applied to a man and his Creator? If this is

confufed

confufed jargon—fay what are the dictates of fober reafon, or the criterions to diftinguifh nonfenfe?

You further farcaftically animadvert on the confiftency of the democratifts, by wrefting the obvious meaning of a common phrafe, *the dregs of the people*; or your contempt for poverty may have led you into an error. Be that as it may, an unprejudiced man would have directly perceived the fingle fenfe of the word, and an old Member of Parliament could fcarcely have miffed it. He who had fo often felt the pulfe of the electors needed not have gone beyond his own experience to dif-cover that the dregs alluded to were the vi-cious, and not the lower clafs of the com-munity.

Again, Sir, I muft doubt your fincerity or your difcernment.—You have been behind the curtain; and, though it might be difficult to bring back your fophifticated heart to nature,

and

and make you feel like a man, yet the awe-
ftruck confufion in which you were plunged
muft have gone off when the vulgar emotion of
wonder, excited by finding yourfelf a Senator,
had fubfided. Then you muft have feen the
clogged wheels of corruption continually oiled
by the fweat of the laborious poor, fqueezed
out of them by unceafing taxation. You muft
have difcovered that the majority in the Houfe
of Commons was often purchafed by the
crown, and that the people were oppreffed by
the influence of their own money, extorted by
the venial voice of a packed reprefentation.

You muft have known that a man of merit
cannot rife in the church, the army, or navy,
unlefs he has fome intereft in a borough; and
that even a paltry excifeman's place can only
be fecured by electioneering intereft. I will
go further, and affert that few Bifhops, though
there have been learned and good Bifhops,
have gained the mitre without fubmitting to

a fervility

a fervility of dependence that degrades the man.—All thefe circumftances you muft have known, yet you talk of virtue and liberty, as the vulgar talk of the letter of the law; and the polite of propriety. It is true that thefe ceremonial obfervances produce decorum; the fepulchres are white wafhed, and do not offend the fqueamifh eyes of high rank; but virtue is out of the queftion when you only worfhip a fhadow, and worfhip it to fecure your property.

Man has been termed, with ftrict propriety, a microcofm, a little world in himfelf.—He is fo; — yet muft, however, be reckoned an ephemera, or, to adopt your figure of rhetoric, a fummer's fly. The perpetuation of property in our families is one of the privileges you moft warmly contend for; but it would not be very difficult to prove that the mind muft have a very limited range that thus confines its benevolence to fuch a narrow circle,

which,

which, with great propriety, may be included in the fordid calculations of blind felf-love.

A brutal attachment to children has appeared moft confpicuous in parents who have treated them like flaves, and demanded due homage for all the property they transferred to them, during their lives. It has led them to force their children to break the moft facred ties ; to do violence to a natural impulfe, and run into legal proftitution to increafe wealth or fhun poverty; and, ftill worfe, the dread of a parental malediction has made many weak characters violate truth in the face of Heaven; and, to avoid a father's angry curfe, the moft facred promifes have been broken.

Who can recount all the unnatural crimes which the *laudable, interefting* defire of perpetuating a name has produced ? The younger children have been facrificed to the eldeft fon; fent into exile, or confined in convents, that they might not encroach on what was called,

with

with fhameful falfehood, the *family* eftate. Will Mr. Burke call this parental affection reafonable or virtuous?—No; it is the fpurious offspring of over-weening, miftaken pride—and not that firft fource of civilization, natural parental affeétion, that makes no difference between child and child, but what reafon juftifies by pointing out fuperior merit.

Another pernicious confequence which arifes from this artificial affeétion is, the infuperable bar which it puts in the way of early marriages. It would be difficult to determine whether the minds or bodies of our youth are moft injured by this impediment. Our young men become felfifh coxcombs, and gallantry with modeft women, and intrigues with thofe of another defcription, weaken both mind and body, before either has arrived at maturity. The charaéter of a mafter of a family, a hufband, and a father, forms the citizen imperceptibly, by producing a fober manlinefs

of

of thought, and orderly behaviour ; but, from
the lax morals and depraved affections of the
libertine, what refults ?—a finical man of tafte,
who is only anxious to fecure his own private
gratifications, and to maintain his rank in
fociety.

The fame fyftem has an equally pernicious
effect on female morals.—Girls are facrificed
to family convenience, or elfe marry to fettle
themfelves in a fuperior rank, and coquet
without reftraint with the fine gentleman
whom I have already defcribed. And to fuch
lengths has this vanity, this defire of fhining,
carried them, that it is not now neceffary to
guard girls againft imprudent love matches;
for if fome widows did not now and then
fall in love, Love and Hymen would feldom
meet, unlefs at a country church.

I do not intend to be farcaftically paradox-
ical when I fay, that a woman of fafhion

takes

takes a hufband that fhe may have it in her power to coquet, the grand bufinefs of genteel life, with a number of admirers, and thus flutter the fpring of life away, without laying up any ftore for the winter of age, or being of any ufe to fociety. Affection in the marriage ftate can only be founded on refpect—and are thefe weak beings refpectable? Children are neglected for lovers, and we exprefs furprife that adulteries are fo common! A woman never forgets to adorn herfelf to make an impreffion on the fenfes of the other fex, and to extort the homage which it is gallant to pay, and yet we wonder that they have fuch confined underftandings!

Have ye not heard that we cannot ferve two mafters; an immoderate defire to pleafe contracts the faculties, and immerges, to borrow the idea of a great philofopher, the foul in matter, till it is unable to mount on the wing of contemplation.

It

It would be an arduous taſk to trace all the vice and miſery that ariſes in ſociety from the middle claſs of people apeing the manners of the great. The grand concern of three parts out of four is to contrive to live above their equals, to appear to be richer than they are; and how much domeſtic comfort and private ſatisfaction is ſacrificed to this irrational ambition! It is a deſtructive mildew that blights the faireſt virtues; benevolence, friendſhip, generoſity, and all thoſe endearing charities which bind human hearts together, and the purſuits which raiſe the mind to higher contemplations, all that were not cankered in the bud by the falſe notions that ' grew with its growth and ſtrengthened with its ſtrength,' are cruſhed by the iron hand of property!

Property, I do not ſcruple to aver it, ſhould be fluctuating, or it is an everlaſting rampart, a barbarous feudal inſtitution, that enables the rich to overpower talents and depreſs virtue.

Beſides,

Befides, an unmanly fervility, moft inimical to true dignity of character is, by thefe means foftered in fociety. Men of fome abilities play on the follies of the rich, and mounting to fortune as they degrade themfelves, they ftand in the way of men of fuperior talents, who cannot advance in fuch dirty fteps, or wade through the filth *they* never boggle at. Purfuing their way ftraight forward, their fpirit is either bent or broken by the rich man's contumelies, or the difficulties they have to encounter.

The only fecurity of property that nature authorifes and reafon fanctions is, the right a man has to enjoy the acquifitions which his talents or induftry have acquired ; and happy would it be for the world if there was no other road to wealth or honour; if pride, in the fhape of parental affection, did not abforb the man. Luxury and effeminacy would not then introduce fo much idiotifm into the noble

families

families which form one of the pillars of our
ſtate. The ground would not lie fallow, nor
would their activity of mind ſpread the con-
tagion of idleneſs, and its concomitant vices,
through the whole maſs of ſociety.

Inſtead of gaming they might nouriſh a virtuous ambition, and love might take place of
the gallantry which you, with knightly fealty,
venerate. Women would then act like mothers, and the fine lady, become a rational
woman, might ſuperintend her family and
ſuckle her children, in order to fulfil her part
of the ſocial compact. The unnatural vices,
produced in the hot-bed of wealth, would
then give place to natural affections, inſtead
" of loſing half their evil by loſing all their
" groſſneſs."—What a ſentiment to come
from a moral pen!

A ſurgeon would tell you that by ſkinning
over a wound you ſpread diſeaſe through
the whole frame; and, ſurely, they indirectly

E   aim

aim at deſtroying all purity of morals, who
poiſon the very ſource of virtue, by ſmearing
a ſentimental varniſh over vice to hide its natural deformity. Stealing, whoring, and drunken-
neſs are groſs vices, I preſume, though they
may not obliterate every moral ſentiment, and
have a vulgar brand that makes them appear
with all their native deformity; but overreach-
ing, adultery, and coquetry, are venial offences,
though they reduce virtue to an empty name,
and make wiſdom conſiſt in ſaving appear-
ances.

‘ On this ſcheme of things [d] a king *is* but a
‘ man ; a queen *is* but a woman; a woman *is*
‘ but an animal, and an animal not of the
‘ higheſt order.’ —All true, Sir ; if ſhe is not
more attentive to the duties of humanity than
faſhionable ladies and queens are in general.
I will ſtill further accede to the opinion you
have ſo juſtly conceived of the ſpirit which

[d] As you ironically obſerve.

begins

begins to animate this age.—' All homage paid
' to the fex in general, as fuch, and without
' diftinct views, is to be regarded as *romance* and
' folly.' Undoubtedly; becaufe fuch homage
vitiates them, prevents their endeavouring to
obtain folid perfonal merit; and, in fhort,
makes thofe beings vain inconfiderate dolls,
who ought to be prudent mothers and ufeful
members of fociety. ' Regicide and facrilege
' are but fictions of fuperftition. corrupting
' jurifprudence, by deftroying its fimplicity.
' The murder of a king, or a queen, or a
' bifhop, are only common homicide.'—Again
I agree with you; but you perceive, Sir, that
by leaving out the word *father*, I think the
comparifon invidious.

You further proceed grofsly to mifreprefent
Dr. Price's meaning; and, with an affectation
of holy fervour, exprefs your indignation at
his profaning a beautiful ejaculation, when al-
luding to the King of France's fubmiflion to

the National Affembly [e]; he rejoiced to hail a glorious revolution, which promifed an univerfal diffufion of liberty and happinefs.

Obferve, Sir, that I called your piety affectation.—A rant to enable you to point your venomous dart, and round your period. I fpeak with warmth, becaufe, of all hypocrites, my foul moft indignantly fpurns a religious one;—and I very cautioufly bring forward fuch a heavy charge to ftrip you of your cloak of fanctity. Your fpeech at the time the bill for a regency was agitated now lies before me.—*Then* you could in direct terms, to promote ambitious or interefted views, exclaim without any pious qualms—' Ought they to ' make a mockery of him, putting a crown ' of thorns on his head, a reed in his hand, ' and dreffing him in a raiment of purple, cry, ' Hail! King of the Britifh!' Where was

[e] In July, when he firft fubmitted to his people; and not the mobbing triumphal cataftrophe in October, which you chofe, to give full fcope to your declamatory powers.

your

your fenfibility when you could utter this cruel mockery, equally infulting to God and man? Go hence, thou flave of impulfe, look into the private receffes of thy heart, and take not a mote from thy brother's eye, till thou haft removed the beam from thine own.

Of your partial feelings I fhall take another view, and fhew that ' the happy effect of fol-
' lowing nature, which is,' you fay, ' wifdom
' without reflection, and *above it*'—has led you into great inconfiftencies, to ufe the fofteft phrafe. When, on a late melancholy occafion, a very important queftion was agitated, with what indecent warmth did you treat a woman, for I fhall not lay any ftrefs on her title, whofe conduct in life has deferved praife, though not, perhaps, the fervile elogiums which have been lavifhed on the queen. But fympathy, and you tell us that you have a heart of flefh, was made to give way to party fpirit and the feelings of a

E 3   man,

man, not to allude to your romantic gallantry, to the views of the ſtateſman. When
you deſcanted on the horrors of the 6th of
October, and gave a glowing, and, in ſome
inſtances, a moſt exaggerated deſcription of
that infernal night, without having troubled yourſelf to clean your palette, you might
have returned home and indulged us with
a ſketch of the miſery you perſonally aggra-
vated.

With what eloquence might you not have
inſinuated, that the ſight of unexpected miſery
and ſtrange reverſe of fortune makes the mind
recoil on itſelf; and, pondering, trace the un-
certainty of all human hope, the frail foundation of ſublunary grandeur! What a climax
lay before you. A father torn from his children,—a huſband from an affectionate wife,—
a man from himſelf! And not torn by the
reſiſtleſs ſtroke of death, for time would then
have lent its aid to mitigate remedileſs ſorrow;
but

but that living death, which only kept hope alive in the corroding form of fufpenfe, was a calamity that called for all your pity.

The fight of auguft ruins, of a depopulated country—what are they to a difordered foul! when all the faculties are mixed in wild confufion. It is then indeed we tremble for humanity—and, if fome wild fancy chance to crofs the brain, we fearfully ftart, and preffing our hand againft our brow, afk if we are yet men?—if our reafon is undifturbed?—if judgment hold the helm? Marius might fit with dignity on the ruins of Carthage, and the wretch in the Baftille, who longed in vain to fee the human face divine, might yet view the operations of his own mind, and vary the leaden profpect by new combinations of thought: poverty, fhame, and even flavery, may be endured by the virtuous man—he has ftill a world to range in—but the lofs of

E 4   reafon

reafon appears a monftrous flaw in the moral world, that eludes all inveftigation, and humbles without enlightening.

In this ftate was the King, when you, with unfeeling difrefpect, and indecent hafte, wifhed to ftrip him of all his hereditary honours.—You were fo eager to tafte the fweets of power, that you could not wait till time had determined, whether a dreadful delirium would fettle into a confirmed madnefs ; but, prying into the fecrets of Omnipotence, you thundered out that God had *hurled him from his throne*, and that it was mockery to recollect that he had been a king. — And who was the monfter whom Heaven had thus awfully depofed, and fmitten with fuch an angry blow ? Surely as harmlefs a character as Lewis XVI.; and our queen, though her heart may not be enlarged by generofity, who will prefume to compare her character with that of the queen of France ?

Where

Where then was the infallibility of that extolled inftinct which rifes above reafon? was
it warped by vanity, or *hurled* from its throne
by felf-intereft? To your own heart anfwer
thefe queftions in the fober hours of reflection
—and, after reviewing this guft of paffion,
learn to refpect the fovereignty of reafon.

I have, Sir, been reading, with a fcrutiniz-
ing, comparative eye, feveral of your infenfi-
ble and profane fpeeches during the King's
illnefs. I difdain to take advantage of a man's
weak fide, or draw confequences from an un-
guarded tranfport—A lion preys not on car-
caffes! But on this occafion you acted fyftema-
tically. It was not the paffion of the moment, over which humanity draws a veil:
No; what but the odious maxims of Machia-
velian policy could have led you to have
fearched in the very dregs of mifery for forcible arguments to fupport your *party*. Had
not vanity or intereft fteeled your heart, you
would

would have been shocked at the cold insen-
sibility which could carry a man to those
dreadful mansions, where human weakness
appears in its most awful form to *calculate* the
chances against his King's recovery. Im-
pressed as you are with respect for royalty, I
am astonished that you did not tremble at every
step, lest Heaven should avenge on your guilty
head the insult offered to its vicegerent. But
the conscience that is under the direction of
transient ebullitions of feeling, is not very
tender or consistent, when the current runs
another way.

Had you been in a philosophizing mood,
had your heart or your reason been at home,
you might have been convinced, by ocular
demonstration, that madness is only the ab-
sence of reason.—The ruling angel had left
its seat, and wild anarchy ensued. You would
have seen that the uncontrouled imagination
often pursues the most regular course in its

3

most

moſt daring flight; and that the eccentricities
are boldly relieved when judgment no longer
officiouſly arranges the ſentiments, by bring-
ing them to the teſt of principles. You would
have ſeen every thing out of nature in that
ſtrange chaos of levity and ferocity, and of all
ſorts of follies jumbled together. You would
have ſeen in that monſtrous tragi-comic ſcene
the moſt oppoſite paſſions neceſſarily ſucceed,
and ſometimes mix with each other in the
mind; alternate contempt and indignation;
alternate laughter and tears; alternate ſcorn
and horror[f]. — This is a true picture of
that chaotic ſtate of mind, called madneſs;
when reaſon gone, we know not where, the
wild elements of paſſion claſh, and all is horror and confuſion. You might have heard
the beſt turned conceits, flaſh following flaſh,
and doubted whether the rhapſody was not

[f] This quotation is not marked with inverted commas,
becauſe it is not exact.

eloquent,

eloquent, if it had not been delivered in an equivocal language, neither verfe nor profe, if the fparkling periods had not ftood alone, wanting force becaufe they wanted concatenation.

It is a proverbial obfervation, that a very thin partition divides wit and madnefs. Poetry is properly addreffed to the imagination, and the language of paffion is with great felicity borrowed from the heightened picture which the imagination draws of fenfible objects concentred by impaffioned reflection. And, during this ' fine phrenfy,' reafon has no right to rein-in the imagination, unlefs to prevent the introduction of fupernumerary images; if the paffion is real, the head will not be ranfacked for ftale tropes and cold rodomontade. I now fpeak of the genuine enthufiafm of genius, which, perhaps, feldom appears, but in the infancy of civilization;

for

for as this advances reafon clips the wing of fancy—the youth becomes a man.

Whether the glory of Europe is fet, I fhall not now enquire; but probably the fpirit of romance and chivalry is in the wane; and reafon will gain by its extinction.

From obferving feveral cold romantic characters I have been led to confine the term romantic to one definition—falfe, or rather artificial, feelings. Works of genius are read with a prepoffeffion in their favour, and fentiments imitated, becaufe they were fafhionable and pretty, and not becaufe they were forcibly felt.

In modern poetry the underftanding and memory often fabricate the pretended effufions of the heart, and romance deftroys all fimplicity; which, in works of tafte, is but a fynonymous word for truth. This romantic fpirit has extended to our profe, and fcattered artificial flowers over the moft barren heath; or a mixture of verfe and profe producing the

7   ftrangeft

ftrangeft incongruities. The turgid bombaft
of fome of your periods fully proves thefe
affertions; for when the heart fpeaks we are
feldom fhocked by hyperbole, or dry raptures.

I fpeak in this decided tone, becaufe from
turning over the pages of your late publica-
tion, with more attention than I did when I
firft read it curforily over, and comparing the
fentiments it contains with your conduct on
many important occafions, I am led very often
to doubt your fincerity, and to fuppofe that you
have faid many things merely for the fake of
faying them well; or to throw fome pointed
obloquy on characters and opinions that joftled
with your vanity.

It is an arduous tafk to follow the doublings
of cunning, or the fubterfuges of inconfiftency;
for in controverfy, as in battle, the brave man
wifhes to face his enemy, and fight on the
fame ground. Knowing, however, the influence

fluence of a ruling paffion, and how often it affumes the form of reafon when there is much fenfibility in the heart, I refpect an opponent, though he tenacioufly maintains opinions in which I cannot coincide; but, if I once difcover that many of thofe opinions are empty rhetorical flourifhes, the refpect is foon changed into that pity which borders on contempt; and the mock dignity and haughty ftalk, only reminds me of the afs in the lion's fkin.

A fentiment of this kind glanced acrofs my mind when I read the following exclamation: ' Whilft the royal captives, who followed in ' the train, were flowly moved along, amidft ' the horrid yells, and fhrilling fcreams, and ' frantic dances, and infamous contumelies, ' and all the unutterable abominations of the ' furies of hell, in the abufed fhape of the ' vileft of women.' Probably you mean women who gained a livelihood by felling vegetables

or

or fifh, who never had had any advantages of
education; or their vices might have loft part
of their abominable deformity, by lofing part
of their groffnefs. The queen of France—
the great and fmall vulgar claim our pity; they
have almoft infuperable obftacles to furmount
in their progrefs towards true dignity of character; but I have fuch a plain downright
underftanding that I do not like to make a
diftinction without a difference.

But it is not very extraordinary that *you*
fhould, for throughout your letter you frequently advert to a fentimental jargon, which
has long been current in converfation, and
even in books of morals, though it never received the *regal* ftamp of reafon. A kind of
myfterious inftinct is *fuppofed* to refide in the
foul, that inftantaneoufly difcerns truth, without the tedious labour of ratiocination. This
inftinct, for I know not what other name to
give it, has been termed *common fenfe,* and

more

more frequently *fenfibility*; and, by a kind of *indefeafible* right, it has been *fuppofed*, for rights of this kind are not eafily proved, to reign paramount· over the other faculties of the mind, and to be an authority from which there is no appeal.

This fubtle magnetic fluid, that runs round the whole circle of fociety, is not fubject to any known rule, or, to ufe ·an obnoxious phrafe, in fpite of the fneers of mock humility, or the timid fears of well-meaning Chriftians, who fhrink from any freedom of thought, left they fhould roufe the old ferpent, to the *eternal fitnefs of things.* It dips, we know not why, granting it to be an infallible inftinct, and, though fuppofed always to point to truth, its pole-ftar ; the point is always fhifting, and feldom ftands due north.

It is to this inftinct, without doubt, that you allude, when you talk of the ' moral ' conftitution of the heart.' To it, I allow, for

F   I confider

I confider it as a congregate of fenfations and paffions, *Poets* muft apply, ' who have to ' deal with an audience not yet graduated in ' the fchool of the rights of men.' They muft, it is clear, often cloud the underftanding, whilft they move the heart by a kind of mechanical fpring; but that ' in the theatre ' the firft intuitive glance' of feeling fhould difcriminate the form of truth, and fee her fair proportion, I muft beg leave to doubt. Sacred be the feelings of the heart! concentred in a glowing flame, they become the fun of life; and, without his invigorating impregnation, reafon would probably lie in helplefs inactivity, and never bring forth her only legitimate offspring—virtue. But to prove that virtue is really an acquifition of the individual, and not the blind impulfe of unerring inftinct, the baftard vice has often been begotten by the fame father.

In

In what refpect are we fuperior to the brute creation, if intellect is not allowed to be the guide of paffion? Brutes hope and fear, love and hate; but, without a capacity to improve, a power of turning thefe paffions to good or evil, they neither acquire virtue nor wifdom. —Why? Becaufe the Creator has not given them reafon[g].

But the cultivation of reafon is an arduous tafk, and men of lively fancy, finding it eafier to follow the impulfe of paffion, endeavour to perfuade themfelves and others that it is moft natural. And happy is it for thofe, who indolently let that heaven-lighted fpark reft like the lamp in fepulchres, that fome virtuous habits, which the reafon of others fhackled them with, fupplies its place. Affection for parents, reverence for fuperiors or

[g] I do not now mean to difcufs the intricate fubject of their mortality; reafon may, perhaps, be given to them in the next ftage of exiftence, if they are to mount in the fcale of life, like men, by the medium of death.

antiquity,

antiquity, notions of honour, or that worldly self-intereſt that ſhrewdly ſhews them that honeſty is the beſt policy: all proceed from the reaſon for which they ſerve as ſubſtitutes; —but it is reaſon at ſecond-hand.

Children are born ignorant, conſequently innocent; the paſſions are neither good nor evil diſpoſitions till they receive a direction, and either bound over the feeble barrier raiſed by a faint glimmering of unexerciſed reaſon, called conſcience, or ſtrengthen her wavering dictates till found principles are deeply rooted, and able to cope with the headſtrong paſſions that often aſſume her awful form. What moral purpoſe can be anſwered by extolling good diſpoſitions, as they are called, when theſe good diſpoſitions are deſcribed as inſtincts: for inſtinct moves in a direct line to its ultimate end, and aſks not for guide or ſupport. But if virtue is to be acquired by experience, or taught by example, reaſon, perfected by reflection,

flection, muſt be the director of the whole
hoſt of paſſions, which produce a fructifying
heat, but no light, that you would exalt into
her place.—She muſt hold the rudder, or, let
the wind blow which way it liſt, the veſſel
will never advance ſmoothly to its deſtined
port; for the time loſt in tacking about would
dreadfully impede its progreſs.

In the name of the people of England, you
ſay, ' that we know *we* have made no diſco-
' veries; and we think that no diſcoveries are
' to be made in morality; nor many in the
' great principles of government, nor in the
' ideas of liberty, which were underſtood long
' before we were born, altogether as well as
' they will be after the grave has heaped its
' mould upon our preſumption, and the ſilent
' tomb ſhall have impoſed its law on our pert
' loquacity. In England we have not yet
' been completely emboweled of our natural
' entrails; we ſtill feel within us, and we

F 3　　　　　' cheriſh

' cherish and cultivate those inbred sentiments
' which are the faithful guardians, the active
' monitors of our duty, the true supporters of
' all liberal and manly morals.'—What do you
mean by inbred sentiments? From whence
do they come? How were they bred? Are
they the brood of folly, which swarm like the
insects on the banks of the Nile, when mud
and putrefaction have enriched the languid soil?
Were these *inbred* sentiments faithful guardians of our duty when the church was an
asylum for murderers, and men worshipped
bread as a God? when slavery was authorised
by law to fasten her fangs on human flesh,
and the iron eat into the very soul? If these
sentiments are not acquired, if our passive
dispositions do not expand into virtuous affections and passions, why are not the Tartars
in the first rude horde endued with sentiments white and *elegant* as the driven snow?
Why is passion or heroism the child of reflection,

flection, the confequence of dwelling with intent contemplation on one object? The appetites are the only perfect inbred powers that I can difcern; and they like inftincts have a certain aim, they can be fatisfied—but improveable reafon has not yet difcovered the perfection it may arrive at.—God forbid!

Firft, however, it is neceffary to make what we know practical. Who can deny, that has marked the flow progrefs of civilization, that men may become more virtuous and happy without any new difcovery in morals? Who will venture to affert that virtue would not be promoted by the more extenfive cultivation of reafon? If nothing more is to be done, let us eat and drink, for to-morrow we die—and die for ever! Who will pretend to fay, that there is as much happinefs diffufed on this globe as it is capable of affording? as many focial virtues as reafon would fofter, if fhe

F 4   could

could gain the ftrength fhe is able to acquire even in this imperfect ftate ?

I am not, Sir, aware of your fneers, hailing a millennium, though a ftate of greater purity of morals may not be a mere poetic fiction; nor did my fancy ever create a heaven on earth, fince reafon threw off her fwaddling clothes. I perceive but too forcibly, that happinefs, literally fpeaking, dwells not here ;—and that we wander to and fro on a vale of darknefs as well as tears. I perceive that my paffions purfue objects that the imagination enlarges, till they become only a fublime idea that fhrinks from the enquiry of fenfe, and mocks the experimental philofophers who would confine this fpiritual phlogifton in their material crucibles. I know that the human underftand is deluded with vain fhadows, and that when we eagerly purfue any ftudy, we only reach the boundary fet to human enquiries.—Thus far fhalt thou go, and no further,

ther, fays fome ftern difficulty; and the caufe
we were purfuing melts into utter darknefs.
But thefe are only the trials of contempla-
tive minds, the foundation of virtue remains
firm.—The power of exercifing our underftanding raifes us above the brutes; and this
exercife produces that ' primary morality,'
which you term ' untaught feelings.'

If virtue be an inftinct, I renounce all hope
of immortality; and with it all the fublime reveries and dignified fentiments that have fmooth-
ed the rugged path of life: it is all a cheat, a
lying vifion; I have difquieted myfelf in vain;
for in my eye all feelings are falfe and fpurious, that do not reft on juftice as their foundation, and are not concentred by univerfal
love.

I reverence the rights of men. — Sacred
rights! for which I acquire a more profound
refpect, the more I look into my own mind;
and, profeffing thefe heterodox opinions, I

ftill

ftill preferve my bowels; my heart is human, beats quick with human fympathies—and I FEAR God!

I bend with awful reverence when I en-quire on what my fear is built.—I fear that fublime power, whofe motive for creating me muft have been wife and good; and I fubmit to the moral laws which my reafon deduces from this view of my dependence on him.— It is not his power that I fear—it is not to an arbitrary will, but to unerring *reafon* I fub-mit.—Submit—yes; I difregard the charge of arrogance to the law that regulates his juft refolves; and the happinefs I pant after muft be the fame in kind, and produced by the fame exertions as his — though unfeigned hu-mility overwhelms every idea that would pre-fume to compare the goodnefs which the moft exalted created being could acquire, with the grand fource of life and blifs.

This fear of God makes me reverence my-felf.

felf.—Yes, Sir, the regard I have for honeſt fame, and the friendſhip of the virtuous, falls far ſhort of the reſpect which I have for my-felf. And this, enlightened ſelf-love, if an epi-thet whoſe meaning has been grofsly perverted will convey my idea, forces me to ſee; and, if I may venture to borrow a proſtituted term, to *feel*, that happineſs is reflected, and that, in communicating good, my foul receives its noble aliment.—I do not trouble myſelf, there-fore, to enquire whether this is the fear the *people* of England feel :—and, if it is *natural* to include all the modifications which you have annexed—it is not.

Befides, I cannot help fufpecting that, if you had the *enlightened* reſpect for yourſelf, which you affect to defpife, you would not have faid that the conſtitution of our church and ſtate, formed, like moſt other modern ones, by de-grees, as Europe was emerging out of barba-rifm, was formed ' under the auſpices, and

' was

' was confirmed by the fanctions, of religion
' and piety.' You have turned over the hiftoric page; have been hackneyed in the ways
of men, and muft know that private cabals
and public feuds, private virtues and vices,
religion and fuperftition, have all concurred to foment the mafs and fwell it to its prefent form; nay more, that it in part owes
its fightly appearance to bold rebellion and
infidious innovation. Factions, Sir, have been
the leaven, and private intereft has produced
public good.

Thefe general reflections are not thrown
out to infinuate that virtue was a creature
of yefterday: No; fhe had her fhare in the
grand drama. I guard' againft mifreprefentation; but the man who cannot modify general affertions, has fcarcely learned the firft
rudiments of reafoning. I know that there is
a great portion of virtue in the Romifh church,
yet I fhould not choofe to neglect clothing
myfelf

myfelf with a garment of my own righteouf-
nefs, depending on a kind donative of works
of fupererogation. I know that there are a
number of clergymen, of all denominations,
wife and virtuous; yet I have not that refpect
for the whole body, which, you fay, charac-
terizes our nation, ' emanating from a certain
' plainnefs and directnefs of underftanding.'
—Now we are ftumbling on *inbred* feelings
and fecret lights again—or, I beg your pardon,
it may be the furbifhed up face which you
choofe to give to the argument.

It is a well-known fact, that when *we*,
the people of England, have a fon whom we
fcarcely know what to do with—*we* make a
clergyman of him. When a living is in the
gift of a family, a fon is brought up to the
church; but not always with hopes full of immortality. ' Such fublime principles are *not*
' *conftantly* infufed into perfons of exalted
' birth;' they fometimes think of '' the pal-
' try

' try pelf of the moment'—and the vulgar care
of preaching the gofpel, or practifing felf-
denial, is left to the poor curates, who, arguing on your ground, cannot have, from the
fcanty ftipend they receive, ' very high and
' worthy notions of their function and deftina-
' tion.' This confecration *for ever*; a word,
that from lips of flesh is big with a mighty
nothing, has not purged the *facred temple* from
all the impurities of fraud, violence, injuftice,
and tyranny. Human paffions ftill lurk in her
fanctum fanctorum; and, without the profane
exertions of reafon, vain would be her ceremonial ablutions; morality would ftill ftand
aloof from this national religion, this ideal
confecration of a ftate; and men would rather
choofe to give the goods of their body, when
on their death beds, to clear the narrow way
to heaven, than reftrain the mad career of
paffion during life.

Such

Such a curious paragraph occurs in this part
of your letter, that I am tempted to tranfcribe
it[h], and muft beg yca to elucidate it, if I mif-
conceive your meaning.

The only way in which the people interfere
in government, religious or civil, is in electing
reprefentatives. And, Sir, let me afk you,

[h] ' When the people have emptied themfelves of all the
' luft of felfifh will, which without religion it is utterly
' impoffible they ever fhould ; when they exercife, and
' exercife perhaps in an higher link of the order of dele-
' gation, the power, which to be legitimate muft be ac-
' cording to that eternal immutable law, in which will and
' reafon are the fame, they will be more careful how they
' place power in bafe and incapable hands. In their no-
' mination to office, they will not appoint to the exercife
' of authority as to a pitiful job, but as to an holy func-
' tion; not according to their fordid felfifh intereft, nor to
' their wanton caprice, nor to their arbitrary will; but
' they will confer that power (which any man may well
' tremble to give or receive) on thofe only, in whom they
' may difcern that predominant proportion of active virtue
' and wifdom, taken together and fitted to the charge,
' fuch as, in the great and inevitable mixed mafs of hu-
' man imperfections and infirmities, is to be found.'

8   with

with manly plainnefs — are thefe *holy* nomi-
nations? Where is the booth of religion?
Does fhe mix her awful mandates, or lift her
perfuafive voice, in thofe fcenes of drunken
riot and beaftly gluttony? Does fhe prefide
over thofe nocturnal abominations which fo
evidently tend to deprave the manners of the
lower · clafs of people? The peftilence ftops
not here — the rich and poor have a common
nature, and many of the great families which,
on this fide adoration, you venerate, date their
mifery, I fpeak of ftubborn matters of fact,
from the thoughtlefs extravagance of an electioneering frolie.—For, after the effervefcence.
of fpirits, raifed by oppofition, and all the little
and tyrannic arts of canvaffing are over —
quiet fouls! they only intended to march rank
and file to fay YES—or NO.

Experience, I believe, will fhew that fordid intereft, or licentious thoughtleffnefs, is
the fpring of action at moft elections.—Again,

I beg

I beg you not to lofe fight of my modifica-
tion of general rules. So far from the people being habitually convinced of the fanctity of the charge they are conferring, the ve-
nality of their votes muft admonifh them that
they have no right to expect difinterefted conduct. But to return to the church, and the
habitual conviction of the people of England.

So far from the people being ' habitually
' convinced that no evil can be acceptable, ei-
' ther in the act or the permiffion, to him whofe
' effence is good;' the fermons which are preached to them are almoft as unintelligible to them
as if they were preached in a foreign tongue.
The language and fentiments rifing above their
capacities, very orthodox Chriftians are driven
to fanatical meetings for amufement, if not for
edification. The clergy, I fpeak of the body,
not forgetting the refpect and affection which
I have for individuals, perform the duty of
their profeffion as a kind of fee-fimple, to

G   entitle

entitle them to the emoluments accruing from it; and their ignorant flock think that merely going to church is meritorious.

So defective, in fact, are our laws, refpecting religious eftablifhments, that I have heard many rational pious clergymen complain, that they had no method of receiving their ftipend that did not clog their endeavours to be ufeful; whilft the lives of many lefs confcientious rectors are paffed in litigious difputes with the people they engaged to inftruct; or in dif-tant cities, in all the eafe of luxurious idlenefs.

But you return to your old firm ground. —*Art thou there, True-penny?* Muft we fwear to fecure property, and make affurance dou-bly fure, to give your perturbed fpirit reft? Peace, peace to the manes of thy patriotic phrenfy, which contributed to deprive fome of thy fellow-citizens of their property in America: another fpirit now walks abroad to fecure the property of the church.—The

tithes

tithes are fafe!—We will not fay for ever—
becaufe the time may come, when the traveller may afk where proud London ftood?
when its temples, its laws, and its trade, may
be buried in one common ruin, and only
ferve as a by-word to point a moral, or furnifh
fenators, who wage a wordy war, on the other
fide of the Atlantic, with tropes to fwell
their thundering burfts of eloquence.

Who fhall dare to accufe you of inconfiftency any more, when you have fo ftaunchly
fupported the defpotic principles which agree
fo perfectly with the unerring intereft of a
large body of your fellow-citizens; not the
largeft—for when you venerate parliaments—I
prefume it is not the majority, for you have had
the prefumption to diffent, and loudly explain
your reafons.—But it was not my intention,
when I began this letter, to defcend to the
minutiæ of your conduct, or to weigh your

G 2   infirmities

infirmities in a balance; it is only fome of your pernicious opinions that I wifh to hunt out of their lurking holes; and to fhew you to yourfelf, ftripped of the gorgeous drapery in which you have enwrapped your tyrannic principles.

That the people of England refpect the national eftablifhment I do not deny; I recollect the melancholy proof which they gave, in this very century, of their *enlightened* zeal and reafonable affection. I likewife know that, according to the dictates of a *prudent* law, in a commercial ftate, truth is reckoned a libel; but I acknowledge, having never made my humanity give place to Gothic gallantry, that I fhould have been better pleafed to have heard that Lord George Gordon was confined on account of the calamities which he brought on his country, than for a *libel* on the queen of France.

But

But one argument which you adduce to ftrengthen your affertion, appears to carry the preponderancy towards the other fide.

You obferve that ' our education is fo formed ' as to confirm and fix this impreffion, (refpect ' for the religious eftablifhment); and that our ' education is in a manner wholly in the hands ' of ecclefiaftics, and in all ftages from in-' fancy to manhood.' Far from agreeing with your, Sir, that thefe regulations render the clergy a more ufeful and refpectable body, ex-perience convinces me that the very contrary is the fact. In fchools and colleges they may, in fome degree, fupport their dignity within the monaftic walls; but, in paying due refpect to the parents of the young nobility under their tutorage, they do not forget, obfequioufly, to refpect their noble patrons. The little re-fpect paid, in great houfes, to tutors and chap-lains proves the fallacy of Mr. Burke's reafon-ing. It would be almoft invidious to remark, that they fometimes are only modern fubfti-

G 3

tutes

tutes for the jefters of Gothic memory, and
ferve as whetftones for the blunt wit of the
noble peer who patronizes them ; and what
refpect a boy can imbibe for a *butt*, at which
the fhaft of ridicule is daily glanced, I leave
thofe to determine who can diftinguifh de-
pravity of morals under the fpecious mafk of
refined manners.

Befides, the cuftom of fending clergymen to
travel with their noble pupils, as humble com-
panions, inftead of exalting, tends inevitably
to degrade the clerical character: it is notorious that they meanly fubmit to the moft
fervile dependence, and glofs over the moft
capricious follies, to ufe a foft phrafe, of the
boys to whom they look up for preferment.
An airy mitre dances before them, and they
wrap their fheep's clothing more clofely about
them, and make their fpirits bend till it is prudent to claim the rights of men and the honeft
freedom of fpeech of an Englifhman. How,
indeed, could they venture to reprove for his

vices

vices their patron: the clergy only give the true feudal emphasis to this word. It has been obferved, by men who have not fuperficially inveftigated the human heart, that when a man makes his fpirit bend to any power but reafon, his character is foon degraded, and his mind fhackled by the very prejudices to which he fubmits with reluctance. The obfervations of experience have been carried ftill further; and the fervility to fuperiors, and tyranny to inferiors, faid to characterize our clergy, have rationally been fuppofed to arife naturally from their affociating with the nobility. 'Among unequals there can be no fociety;'—giving a manly meaning to the term, from fuch intimacies friendfhip can never grow; if the bafis of friendfhip is mutual refpect, and not a commercial treaty. Taken thus out of their fphere, and enjoying their tithes at a diftance from their flocks, is it not natural for them to become courtly parafites, and intriguing dependents on great patrons, or the

G 4   treafury?

treafury ? Obferving all this—for thefe things have not been tranfacted in the dark—our young men of fafhion, by a common, though erroneous, affociation of ideas, have conceived a contempt for religion, as they fucked in with their milk a contempt for the clergy.

The people of England, Sir, in the thirteenth and fourteenth centuries, I will not go any further back to infult the afhes of departed popery, did not fettle the eftablifhment, and endow it with princely revenues, to make it proudly rear its head, as a part of the conftitutional body, to guard the liberties of the community; but, like fome of the laborious commentators on Shakefpeare, you have affixed a meaning to laws that chance, or, to fpeak more philofophically, the interefted views of men, fettled, not dreaming of your ingenious elucidations.

What, but the rapacity of the only men who exercifed their reafon, the priefts, fecured fuch vaft property to the church, when a man

gave

gave his perifhable fubftance to fave himfelf from the dark torments of purgatory, and found it more convenient to indulge his depraved appetites, and pay an exorbitant price for abfolution, than liften to the fuggeftions f reafon, and work out his own falvati on: in a word, was not the feparation of religion from morality the work of the priefts, and partly achieved in thofe *honourable* days which you fo pioufly deplore?

That civilization, that the cultivation of the underftanding, and refinement of the affections, naturally makes a man religious, I am proud to acknowledge.—What elfe can fill the aching void in the heart, that human pleafures, human friendfhips can never fill? What elfe can render us refigned to live, though condemned to ignorance?—What but a profound reverence for the model of all perfection, and the myfteriou's tie which arifes from a love of goodnefs? What can make us

reverence

reverence ourfelves, but a reverence for that Being, of whom we are a faint image? That mighty Spirit moves on the waters—confufion hears his voice, and the troubled heart ceafes to beat with anguifh, for truft in Him bade it be ftill. Confcious dignity may make us rife fuperior to calumny, and fternly brave the winds of adverfe fortune, raifed in our own efteem by the very ftorms of which we are the fport— but when friends are unkind, and the heart has not the prop on which it fondly leaned, where can the tender fuffering being fly but to the Searcher of hearts? and, when death has defolated the prefent fcene, and torn from us the friend of our youth—when we walk along the accuftomed path, and, almoft fancying nature dead, afk, Where art thou who gave life to thefe well-known fcenes? when memory heightens former pleafures to contraft our prefent profpects—there is but one fource of comfort within our reach ;—and in this fublime

6   folitude

folitude the world appears to contain only the Creator and the creature, of whofe happinefs he is the fource.—Thefe are human feelings; but I know not of any common nature or common relation amongft men but what refults from reafon. The common affections and paffions equally bind brutes together; and it is only the continuity of thofe relations that entitles us to the denomination of rational creatures; and this continuity arifes from reflection—from the operations of that reafon which you contemn with flippant difrefpect.

If then it appears, arguing from analogy, that reflection muft be the natural foundation of our *rational* affections, and of that experience which enables one man to rife above another, a phenomenon that has never been feen in the brute creation, it may not be ftretching the argument further than it will go to fuppofe, that thofe men who are obliged to exercife their reafon have the moft reafon, and are

the

the perfons pointed out by Nature to direct the fociety of which they make a part, on any extraordinary emergency.

Time only will fhew whether the general cenfure, which you afterwards qualify, if not contradict, and the unmerited contempt that you have oftentatioufly difplayed of the National Affembly, is founded on reafon, the off-fpring of conviction, or the fpawn of envy. Time may fhew, that this obfcure throng knew more of the human heart and of legifla-tion than the profligates of rank, emafculated by hereditary effeminacy.

It is not, perhaps, of very great confequence who were the founders of a ftate; favages, thieves, curates, or practitioners in the law. It is true that you might farcaftically remark, that the Romans had always a *fmack* of the old leaven, and that the private robbers, fup-pofing the tradition to be true, only became public depredators. You might have added, that

that their civilization muft have been very
partial, and had more influence on the manners than morals of the people; or the amufe-
ments of the amphitheatre would not have
remained an everlafting blot not only on
their humanity, but on their refinement, if a
vicious elegance of behaviour and luxurious
mode of life is not a proftitution of the term.
However, the thundering cenfures which you
have caft with a ponderous arm, and the more
playful bufhfiring of ridicule, are not arguments that will ever depreciate the National
Affembly, for applying to their underftanding
rather than to their imagination, when they
met to fettle the newly acquired liberty of the
ftate on a folid foundation.

If you had given the fame advice to a young
hiftory painter of abilities, I fhould have ad-
mired your judgment, and re-echoed your fentiments. Study, you might have faid, the
noble models of antiquity, till your imagination

tion is inflamed; and, rifing above the vulgar practice of the hour, you may imitate without copying thofe great originals. A glowing picture, of fome interefting moment, would probably have been produced by thefe natural means; particularly if one little circumftance is not overlooked, that the painter had noble models to revert to, calculated to excite admiration and ftimulate emulative exertions.

But, in fettling a conftitution that involved the happinefs of millions, that ftretch beyond the computation of fcience, it was, perhaps, neceffary to have a higher model in view than the *imagined* virtues of their forefathers, and wife to deduce their refpect for themfelves from the only legitimate fource, refpect for juftice. Why was it a duty to repair an ancient caftle, built in barbarous ages, of Gothic materials? why were they obliged to rake amongft heterogeneous ruins; or rebuild old walls, whofe foundations could fcarcely be explored,

plored, when a fimple ftructure might be raifed on the foundation of experience, the only valuable inheritance our forefathers can bequeath ? But of this bequeft we can make little ufe till we have gained a ftock of our own ; and, even then, the inherited experience would rather ferve as light-houfes, to warn us againft dangerous rocks or fand-banks, than as pofts that ftand at every turning to point out the right road.

Nor was it abfolutely neceffary that they fhould be diffident of themfelves when they could not difcern, or were not at the trouble to feek for the *almoft obliterated* conftitution of their anceftors. They fhould firft have been convinced that our conftitution was not only the beft modern, but the beft poffible one ; and that our focial compact was the fureft foundation of all the *poffible* liberty a mafs of men could enjoy, that the human underftanding could form. They fhould have been certain that

our

our reprefentation anfwered all the purpofes of reprefentation; and that an eftablifhed inequality of rank and property fecured the liberty of the whole community, inftead of rendering it a founding epithet of fubjection, when applied to the nation at large. They fhould have had the fame refpect for our Houfe of Commons that you, vauntingly, intrude on us, though your conduct throughout life has fpoken a very different language.

That the Britifh Houfe of Commons is filled with every thing illuftrious in rank, in defcent, in hereditary, and acquired opulence, may be true,—but that it contains every thing refpectable in talents, in military, civil, naval, and political diftinction, is very problematical. Arguing from natural caufes, the very contrary would appear to the fpeculatift to be the fact; and let experience fay whether thefe fpeculations are built on fure ground.

It

It is true you lay great ſtreſs on the effects produced by the idea of a liberal deſcent; but from the conduct of men of rank, men of diſcernment would rather be led to conclude, that this idea obliterated inſtead of inſpiring native dignity, and ſubſtituted a factitious pride that diſemboweled the man. The liberty of the rich has its enſigns armorial to puff the individual out with unſubſtantial honours; but where are blazoned the ſtruggles of virtuous poverty? Who, indeed, would dare to blazon what would blur the pompous monumental inſcription, and make us view with horror, as monſters in human ſhape, the ſuperb gallery of portraits thus proudly ſet in battle array.

But to examine the ſubject more cloſely. Is it among the liſt of poſſibilities that a man of rank and fortune *can* have received a good education? How can he diſcover that he is a man, when all his wants are inſtantly ſup-

H   plied,

plied, and invention is never sharpened by necessity? Will he labour, for every thing valuable must be the fruit of laborious exertions, to attain knowledge and virtue, in order to merit the affection of his equals, when the flattering attention of sycophants is a more luscious cordial?

Health can only be secured by temperance; but is it easy to persuade a man to live on plain food even to recover his health, who has been accustomed to fare sumptuously every day? Can a man relish the simple food of friendship, who has been habitually pampered by flattery? And when the blood boils, and the senses meet allurements on every side, will knowledge be pursued on account of its abstract beauty? No; it is well known that talents are only to be unfolded by industry, and that we must have made some advances, led by an inferior motive, before we discover that they are their own reward.

But

But *full blown* talents *may,* according to
your fyftem, be hereditaty, and as independent of ripening judgment, as the inbred feelings that, rifing above reafon, naturally guard
Englifhmen from error. Noble franchifes!
what a grovelling mind muft that man have,
who can pardon his ftep-dame Nature for not
having made him at leaft a lord!

And who will, after this defcription of fe-
natorial virtues, dare to fay that our Houfe of
Commons has often refembled a bear-garden;
and appeared rather like a committee of *ways
and means* than a dignified legiflative body,
though the concentrated wifdom and virtue of
the whole nation blazed in one fuperb con-
ftellation? That it contains a dead weight of
benumbing opulence I readily allow, and of
ignoble ambition; nor is there any thing fur-
paffing belief in a fuppofition that the raw re-
cruits, when properly drilled by the minifter,
would gladly march to the Upper Houfe to

unite

unite hereditary honours to fortune. But talents, knowledge, and virtue, muſt be a part of the man, and cannot be put, as robes of ſtate often are, on a ſervant or a block, to render a pageant more magnificent.

Our Houſe of Commons, it is true, has been celebrated as a ſchool of eloquence, a hot-bed for wit, even when party intrigues narrow the underſtanding and contract the heart; yet, from the few proficients it has accompliſhed, this inferior praiſe is not of great magnitude: nor of great conſequence, Mr. Locke would have added, who was ever of opinion that eloquence was oftener employed to make ' the worſe appear the better ' part,' than to ſupport the dictates of cool judgment. However, the greater number who have gained a ſeat by their fortune and hereditary rank, are content with their pre-eminence, and ſtruggle not for more hazardous honours. But you are an exception; you

have

have raifed yourfelf by the exertion of abilities, and thrown the automatons of rank into
the back ground. It is in you a generous
conteft for fecondary honours, or a grateful
tribute of refpect due to the noble afhes
that lent a hand to raife you into notice, by
introducing you into the houfe you have
ever been an ornament to, if not a fupport.
But unfortunately you have lately loft a great
part of your popularity: members were tired
of liftening to declamation, or had not fufficient tafte to be amufed when you ingenioufly
wandered from the queftion, and faid certainly many good things, if they were not to
the prefent purpofe. You were the Cicero of
one fide of the houfe for feveral years; and
then to fink into oblivion, to fee your bloom-
ing honours fade before you, was enough to
roufe all that was human in you—and, producing thefe impaffioned *Reflections*, has been
a glorious revivification — Richard is him-

H 3   felf

felf again! He is ftill a great man, though he has deferted his poft, and buried in elogiums, on church eftablifhments, the enthufiafm that forced him to throw the weight of his talents on the fide of liberty and natural rights, when the *will* of the nation oppreffed the Americans.

There appears to be fuch a mixture of real fenfibility and fondly cherifhed romance in your compofition, that the prefent crifis carries you out of yourfelf; and fince you could not be one of the grand movers, the next *beft* thing that dazzled your imagination was to be a confpicuous oppofer. Full of yourfelf, you make as much noife to convince the world that you defpife the revolution, as Rouffeau did to perfuade his contemporaries to let him live in obfcurity.

Reading your Reflections warily over, it has continually and forcibly ftruck me, that had you been a Frenchman, you would have been,

6   in

in fpite of your refpeƈt for rank and antiquity,
a violent revolutioniſt; and deceived, as you
now probably are, by the paſſions that cloud
your reafon, have termed your romantic en-
thuſiaſm an enlightened love of your country,
a refpeƈt for the rights of men. Your imagination would have taken fire, and have found
arguments, full as ingenious as thoſe you now
offer, to prove that the conſtitution, of which
fo few pillars remained, that conſtitution
which time had almoſt obliterated, was not a
model fufficiently noble to deſerve cloſe ad-
herence. And, for the Engliſh conſtitution,
you might not have had ſuch a profound veneration as you have lately acquired; nay, it
is not impoſſible but you might have enter-
tained the fame opinion of the Engliſh Parliament, that you profeſſed to have during the
American war.

Another obſervation which, by frequently oc-
curring, has almoſt grown into a conviƈtion, is

H 4
fimply

fimply this, that had the Englifh in general repro-
bated the French revolution, you would have
ftood forth alone, and been the avowed Goliah of
liberty. But, not liking to fee fo many brothers
near the throne of fame, you have turned the
current of your paffions, and confequently of
your reafoning, another way. Had Dr. Price's
fermon not lighted fome fparks very like envy
in your bofom, I fhrewdly fufpect that he would
have been treated with more candour; nor is
it charitable to fuppofe that any thing but
perfonal pique and hurt vanity could have
dictated fuch bitter farcafms and reiterated ex-
preffions of contempt.

But without fixed principles even goodnefs
of heart is no fecurity from inconfiftency, and
mild affectionate fenfibility only renders a man
more ingeniously cruel, when the pangs of
hurt vanity are miftaken for virtuous indignation, and the gall of bitternefs for the milk
of Chriftian charity.

Where

Where is the dignity, the infallibility of
fenfibility, in the fair ladies, whom, if the
voice of rumour is to be credited, the captive
negroes curfe in all the agony of bodily pain,
for the unheard of tortures they invent? It is
probable that fome of them, after a flagella-
tion, compofe their ruffled fpirits and exercife their tender feelings by the perufal of the
laft new novel.—How true thefe tears are to
nature, I leave you to determine. But thefe
ladies may have read your Enquiries concern-
ing the origin of our ideas of the Sublime and
Beautiful, and, convinced by your arguments,
have laboured to be pretty, by counterfeiting
weaknefs.

You may have convinced them that *little-
nefs* and weaknefs are the very effence of
beauty; and that the Supreme Being, in
giving women beauty in the moft fuperemi-
nent degree, feemed to command them, by the
powerful voice of Nature, not to cultivate the

moral

moral virtues that might chance to excite respect, and interfere with the pleasing sensations they were created to inspire. Confining thus truth, fortitude, and humanity, within the rigid pale of manly morals, they might justly argue, that to be loved, woman's high end and great distinction! they should ' learn to ' lisp, to totter in their walk,' and nick-name God's creatures. Never, they might repeat after you, was any man, much less a woman, rendered amiable by the force of those exalted qualities, fortitude, justice, wisdom, and truth; and thus forewarned of the sacrifice they must make to those austere, unnatural virtues, they would be authorised to turn all their attention to their persons, systematically neglecting morals to secure beauty.— Some rational old woman might chance to stumble at this doctrine, and hint, that in avoiding atheism you had not steered clear of the mussulman's creed; but you could readily

exculpate

exculpate yourfelf by turning the charge on Nature, who made our idea of beauty independent of reafon. Nor would it be neceffary for you to recollect, that if virtue has any other foundation than worldly utility, you have clearly proved that one half of the human fpecies, at leaft, have not fouls ; and that Nature, by making women little, fmooth, delicate, fair creatures, never defigned that they fhould exercife their reafon to acquire the virtues that produce oppofite, if not contradictory, feelings. The affection produced by them, to be uniform and perfect, fhould not be tinctured with the refpect moral virtues infpire, left pain fhould be blended with pleafure, and admiration difturb the foft intimacy of love. This laxity of morals in the female world is certainly more captivating to a libertine imagination than the cold arguments of reafon, that give no fex to virtue. If beautiful weaknefs was interwoven in a woman's frame, if

the

the chief bufinefs of her life is to infpire love, and Nature has made an eternal diftinction between the qualities that dignify a rational being and this animal perfection, her duty and happinefs in this life muft clafh with any preparation for a more exalted ftate. So that Plato and Milton were grofsly miftaken in afferting that human love led to heavenly, and was only an exaltation of the fame affection; for the love of the Deity, which is mixed with the moft profound reverence, muft be love of perfection, and not compaffion for weaknefs.

To fay the truth, I not only tremble for the fouls of women, but for the good natured man, whom every one loves. The *amiable* weaknefs of their minds is a ftrong argument againft its immateriality, and feems to prove that beauty relaxes the *folids* of the foul as well as the body.

It follows then immediately, from your own reafoning, that refpect and love are an-

tagonift

tagoniſt principles; and that, if we really
wiſh to render men more virtuous, we muſt
endeavour to baniſh all enervating modifications of beauty from civil ſociety. We muſt,
only to carry your argument a little further,
return to the Spartan regulations, and ſettle
the virtues of men on the ſtern foundation of
mortification and ſelf-denial; for any attempt
to civilize the heart, to make it humane by
implanting reaſonable principles, is a mere
philoſophic dream. If refinement inevitably
leſſens reſpect for virtue, by rendering beauty
the grand tempter, more ſeductive; if theſe
relaxing feelings are incompatible with the
nervous exertions of morality, the ſun of Europe is not ſet; it begins to dawn, when cold
metaphyſicians try to make the head give laws
to the heart.

But ſhould experience prove that there is a
beauty in virtue, a charm in order, which
neceſſarily implies exertion, a depraved ſen-
ſual taſte may give way to a more manly one
—and

—and *melting* feelings to rational fatisfactions. Both may be equally natural to man ; the teft is their moral difference, and that point reafon alone can decide.

Such a glorious change can only be produced by liberty. Inequality of rank muft ever impede the growth of virtue, by vitiating the mind that fubmits or domineers; that is ever employed to procure nourifhment for the body, or amufement for the mind. And if this grand example is fet by an affembly of unlettered clowns, if they can produce a crifis that may involve the fate of Europe, and ' more than Europe,' you muft allow us to refpect unfophifticated common fenfe, and reverence the active exertions that were not relaxed by a faftidious refpect for the beauty of rank, or the dread of the deformity produced by a void in the focial ftructure.

After your contemptuous manner of fpeaking of the National Affembly, after defcanting on the coarfe vulgarity of their proceed-

ings, which, according to your own definition of virtue, is a proof of its genuinenefs;
was it not a little inconfiftent, not to fay ab-
furd, to affert, that a dozen people of quality
were not a fufficient counterpoife to the vulgar mob with whom they condefcended to
affociate? Have we half a dozen leaders of
eminence in our Houfe of Commons, or even
in the fafhionable world? yet the fheep obfequioufly purfue their fteps with all the unde-
viating fagacity of inftinct.

In order that liberty fhould have a firm
foundation, an acquaintance with the world
would naturally lead cool men to conclude
that it muft be laid, knowing the weaknefs of
the human heart, and the ' deceitfulnefs of
' riches,' either by *poor* men or philofophers,
if a fufficient number of men, difinterefted
from principle, or truly wife, could be found.
Was it natural to expect that fenfual prejudices fhould give way to reafon, or prefent

feelings

feelings to enlarged views?—No; I am afraid
that human nature is ſtill in ſuch a weak ſtate,
that the abolition of titles, the corner-ſtone of
deſpotiſm, could only have been the work of
men who had no titles to ſacrifice. The National Aſſembly, it is true, contains ſome honourable exceptions; but the majority had not
ſuch powerful feelings to ſtruggle with, when
reaſon led them to reſpect the naked dignity
of virtue.

Weak minds are always timid. And what
can equal the weakneſs of mind produced by
ſervile flattery, and the vapid pleaſures that
neither hope nor fear ſeaſoned ? Had the conſtitution of France been new modelled, or more
cautiouſly repaired, by the lovers of elegance
and beauty, it is natural to ſuppoſe that the
imagination would have erected a fragile temporary building, or the power of one tyrant,
divided amongſt a hundred, might have rendered the ſtruggle for liberty only a choice of
maſters.

mafters. And the glorious *chance* that now is given to human nature of attaining more virtue and happinefs than has hitherto bleffed our globe, might have been facrificed to a meteor of the imagination, a bubble of paffion.

But the ecclefiaftics would probably have remained in quiet poffeffion of their fine-cures; your gall might not have been mixed with your ink on account of this daring facrilege. The nobles would have had bowels for their younger fons, if not for the mifery of their fellow-creatures. An auguft mafs of property would have been tranfmitted to pofterity to guard the temple of fuperftition, and prevent reafon from entering with her officious light. The pomp of religion would have continued to imprefs the fenfes, if fhe was unable to fubjugate the paffions.

Is hereditary weaknefs neceffary to render religion lovely? and will her form have loft the fmooth delicacy that infpires love, when

I   ftripped

ftripped of its Gothic drapery? Muft every grand model be placed on the pedeftal of property? and is there no beauteous proportion in virtue, when not clothed in a fenfual garb?

Of thefe queftions there would be no end, though they lead to the fame conclufion;— that your politics and morals, when fimplified, would undermine religion and virtue to fet up a fpurious, fenfual beauty, that has long debauched your imagination, under the fpecious form of natural feelings.

And what is this mighty revolution in property? The prefent incumbents only are injured, or the hierarchy of the clergy, an ideal part of the conftitution, which you have perfonified, to render your affection more tender. How has pofterity been injured by a diftribution of the property fnatched, perhaps, from innocent hands, but accumulated by the moft abominable violation of every fentiment of juftice and piety! Was the

6   monument

monument of former ignorance and iniquity
to be held facred, to enable the prefent poffeffors of enormous benefices to *diffolve* in
indolent pleafures? Was not their convenience, for they have not been turned adrift on
the world, to give place to a juft partition of
the land belonging to the ftate? And did not
the refpeét due to the natural equality of man
require this triumph over Monkifh rapacity?
Were thofe monfters to be reverenced on account of their antiquity, and their unjuft
claims perpetuated to their ideal children, the
clergy, merely to preferve the facred majefty
of Property inviolate, and to enable the Church
to retain her priftine fplendor? Can pofterity
be injured by individuals lofing the chance of
obtaining great wealth, without meriting it,
by its being diverted from a narrow channel, and difembogued into the fea that affords
clouds to water all the land? Befides, the
clergy not brought up with the expeétation of

great

great revenues will not feel the·lofs; and if
bifhops fhould happen to be chofen on account of their perfonal merit, religion may be
benefited by the vulgar nomination.

The fophiftry of afferting that Nature leads
us to reverence our civil inftitutions from the
fame principle that we venerate aged individuals, is a palpable fallacy ' that is fo like truth,
' it will ferve the turn as well.' And when
you add, ' that we have chofen our nature
' rather than our fpeculations, our breafts ra-
' ther than our inventions,' the pretty jargon
feems equally unintelligible.

But it was the downfall of the vifible power
and dignity of the church that roufed your ire;
you could have excufed a little fqueezing of
the individuals to fupply prefent exigencies;
the actual poffeffors of the property might
have been oppreffed with fomething like im-
punity, if the church had not been fpoiled of
its gaudy trappings. You love the church,
your

your country, and its laws, you repeatedly tell us, becaufe they deferve to be loved; but from you this is not a panegyric: weaknefs and indulgence are the only incitements to love and confidence that you can difcern, and it cannot be denied that the tender mother you venerate deferves, on this fcore, all your affection.

It would be as vain a tafk to attempt to obviate all your paffionate objections, as to unravel all your plaufible arguments, often illuftrated by known truths, and rendered forcible by pointed invectives. I only attack the foundation. On the natural principles of juftice I build my plea for diffeminating the property artfully faid to be appropriated to religious purpofes, but, in reality, to fupport idle tyrants, amongft the fociety whofe anceftors were cheated or forced into illegal grants. Can there be an opinion more fubverfive of morality, than that time fanctifies crimes, and filences the blood that calls out for retribution, if not for vengeance? If the

I 3   revenue

revenue annexed to the Gallic church was greater than the moſt bigotted proteſtant would now allow to be its reaſonable ſhare, would it not have been trampling on the rights of men to perpetuate ſuch an arbitrary appropriation of the common ſtock, becauſe time had rendered the fraudulent ſeizure venerable? Beſides, if Reaſon had ſuggeſted, as ſurely ſhe muſt, if the imagination had not been allowed to dwell on the faſcinating pomp of ceremonial grandeur, that the clergy would be rendered both more virtuous and uſeful by being put more on a par with each other, and the maſs of the people it was their duty to inſtruct;—where was there room for heſitation? The charge of preſumption, thrown by you on the moſt reaſonable innovations, may, without any violence to truth, be retorted on every reformation that has meliorated our condition, and even on the improveable faculty that gives us a claim to the pre-eminence of intelligent beings.

Plauſibility,

Plaufibility, I know, can only be unmafked by fhewing the abfurdities it gloffes over, and the fimple truths it involves with fpecious errors. Eloquence has often confounded triumphant villany; but it is probable that it has more frequently rendered the boundary that feparates virtue and vice doubtful.—Poifons may be only medicines in judicious hands; but they fhould not be adminiftered by the ignorant, becaufe they have fometimes feen great cures performed by their powerful aid.

The many fenfible remarks and pointed obfervations which you have mixed with opinions that ftrike at our deareft interefts, fortifies thofe opinions, and gives them a degree of ftrength that renders them formidable to the wife, and convincing to the fuperficial. It is impoffible to read half a dozen pages of your book without admiring your ingenuity, or indignantly fpurning your fophifms. Words

I 4   are

are heaped on words, till the underſtanding is confuſed by endeavouring to diſentangle the ſenſe, and the memory by tracing contradiç-tions. After obſerving a hoſt of theſe contra-dictions, it can ſcarcely be a breach of charity to think that you have often ſacrificed your ſincerity to enforce your favourite arguments, and called in your judgment to adjuſt the arrangement of words that could not convey its dictates.

A fallacy of this kind, I think, could not have eſcaped you, when you were treating the ſubject that called forth your bittereſt animad-verſions, the confiſcation of the eccleſiaſtical revenue. Who of the vindicators of the rights of men ever ventured to aſſert, that the clergy of the preſent day ſhould be puniſhed on ac-count of the intolerable pride and inhuman cruelty of many of their predeceſſors? No; ſuch a thought never entered the mind of thoſe who warred with inveterate prejudices.

A deſperate

A defperate difeafe required a powerful remedy. Injuftice had no right to reft on prefcription ; nor has the character of the prefent clergy any weight in the argument.

You find it very difficult to feparate policy from juftice : in the political world they have frequently been feparated with fhameful dex-terity. To mention a recent inftance. According to the limited views of timid, or in-terefted politicians, an abolition of the infernal flave trade would not only be unfound policy, but a flagrant infringement of the laws (though they are allowed to have been infamous) that authorife the planters to purchafe their eftates. But is it not confonant with juftice, with the common principles of humanity, not to men-tion Chriftianity, to abolifh this abominable inveterate mifchief ? There is not one ar-

gument,

¹ ' When men are encouraged to go into a certain
' mode of life by the exifting laws, and protected in that
' mode as in a lawful occupation—when they have ac-
' commodated

gument, one invective, levelled by you at the confiscators of the church revenue, which could not, with the strictest propriety, be applied by the planters and negro-drivers to our Parliament, if it gloriously dared to shew the world that British senators were men : if the naturaltfeelings of humanity silenced the cold cautions of timidity, till this stigma on our nature was wiped off, and all men were allowed to enjoy their birth-right—liberty, till by their crimes they had authorised society to deprive them of the blessing they had abused.

The same arguments might be used in India, if any attempt was made to bring back things to nature, to prove that a man ought

'commodated *all their ideas, and all their habits to it,*' &c.—' I am sure it is unjust in legislature, by an arbitrary
' act, to offer a sudden violence to their minds and their
' feelings; forcibly to degrade them from their state and
' condition, and to stigmatize with shame and infamy that
' character and those customs which before had been made
' the measure of their happiness.'

never

never to quit the profeffion of his lineal forefathers. The Bramins would doubtlefs find
many ingenious reafons to juftify this debafing,
though venerable prejudice; and would not,
it is to be fuppofed, forget to obferve that
time, by interweaving the oppreffive law with
many ufeful cuftoms, had rendered it for the
prefent very convenient, and confequently
legal. Almoft every vice that has degraded
our nature might be juftified by fhewing that
it had been productive of *fome* benefit to fociety: for it would be as difficult to point out
pofitive evil as unallayed good, in this imperfect ftate. What indeed would become of
morals, if they had no other teft than prefcription? The manners of men may change
without end; but, wherever reafon receives
the leaft cultivation—wherever men rife above
brutes, morality muft reft on the fame bafe.
And the more man difcovers of the nature of
his mind and body, the more clearly he is
convinced,

convinced, that to act according to the dictates of reason is to conform to the will of God.

The test of honour may be arbitrary and fallacious, and, retiring into subterfuge, elude close enquiry; but true morality shuns not the day, nor shrinks from the ordeal of investigation. Most of the happy revolutions that have taken place in the world have happened when weak princes held the reins they could not manage; but are they, on that account, to be canonized as saints or demi-gods, and pushed forward to notice on the throne of ignorance? Pleasure wants a zest, if experience cannot compare it with pain; but who courts pain to heighten his pleasures? A transient view of society will further illustrate arguments that appear so obvious. I am almost ashamed to produce illustrations. How many children have been taught œconomy, and many other virtues, by the extravagant thoughtlessness of their parents; yet a good education is allowed to be

an

an ineftimable blefling. The tendereft mothers are often the moft unhappy wives; but
can the good that accrues from the private
diftrefs that produces a fober dignity of mind
juftify the inflictor? Right or wrong may be
eftimated according to the point of fight, and
other adventitious circumftances; but, to difcover its real nature, the enquiry muft go
deeper than the furface, and beyond the local
confequences that confound good and evil together. But the rich and weak, a numerous
train, will certainly applaud your fyftem, and
loudly celebrate your pious reverence for authority and eftablifhments—they find it plea-
fanter to enjoy than to think; to juftify oppreffion than correct abufes.—*The rights of
men* is a grating found that fets their teeth on
edge; the impertinent enquiry of philofophic
meddling innovation. If the poor are in diftrefs, they will make fome *benevolent* exertions
to affift them; they will confer obligations,
but

but not do juftice. Benevolence is a very
amiable fpecious quality; yet the averfion
which men feel to accept a right as a favour,
fhould rather be extolled as a veftige of native
dignity, than ftigmatized as the odious off-
fpring of ingratitude. The poor confider the
rich as their lawful prey; but we ought not
too feverely to animadvert on their ingratitude.
When they receive an alms they are commonly grateful at the moment; but old habits quickly return, and cunning has ever
been a fubftitute for force.

That both phyfical and moral evil were not
only forefeen, but entered into the fcheme of
Providence, when this world was contem-
plated in the Divine mind, who can doubt,
without robbing Omnipotence of a moft exalted
attribute? But the bufinefs of the life of a
good man fhould be, to feparate light from
darknefs; to diffufe happinefs, whilft he fubmits to unavoidable mifery. And a conviction

tion that there is much unavoidable wretched-
nefs, appointed by the grand Difpofer of all
events, fhould not flacken his exertions: the
extent of what is poffible can only be difcerned
by God. The juftice of God may be vindi-
cated by a belief in a future ftate; but, only by
believing that evil is educing good for the individual, and not for an imaginary whole. The
happinefs of the whole muft arife from the happinefs of the conftituent parts, or the effence of
juftice is facrificed to a fuppofed grand arrangement. And that may be good for the
whole of a creature's exiftence, that difturbs the
comfort of a fmall portion. The evil which
an individual fuffers for the good of the community is partial, it muft be allowed, if the
account is fettled by death.—But the partial
evil which it fuffers, during one ftage of exiftence, to render another ftage more perfect, is
ftrictly juft. The Father of all only can regu-
late the education of his children. To fuppofe

poſe that, during the whole or part of its exiſtence, the happineſs of any individual is
ſacrificed to promote the welfare of ten, or
ten thouſand, other beings—is impious. But
to ſuppoſe that the happineſs, or animal enjoy-
ment, of one portion of exiſtence is ſacrificed
to improve and ennoble the being itſelf, and
render it capable of more perfect happineſs, is
not to reflect on either the goodneſs or wiſdom of God.

It may be confidently aſſerted that no man
chooſes evil, becauſe it is evil; he only miſtakes it for happineſs, the good he ſeeks. And
the deſire of rectifying theſe miſtakes, is the
noble ambition of an enlightened underſtanding, the impulſe of feelings that Philoſophy
invigorates. To endeavour to make unhappy
men reſigned to their fate, is the tender endeavour of ſhort-ſighted benevolence, of tranſient
yearnings of humanity; but to labour to
increaſe human happineſs by extirpating error,

is

is a mafculine godlike affection. This remark
may be carried ftill further. Men who poffefs
uncommon fenfibility, whofe quick emotions
fhew how clofely the eye and heart are con-
nected, foon forget the moft forcible fenfations. Not being reflected on, nor tarrying
long in the brain, the next fenfations, of
courfe, obliterated them. Memory, however,
treafures up thefe proofs of native goodnefs;
and the being who is not fpurred on to any
virtuous act, ftill thinks itfelf of confequence,
and boafts of its feelings. Why? Becaufe the
fight of diftrefs, or an affecting narrative, made
its blood flow with more velocity, and the
heart, literally fpeaking, beat with fympathetic
emotion. We ought to beware of confound-
ing mechanical inftinctive fenfations with
emotions that reafon deepens, and juftly terms
the feelings of humanity. This word difcri-
minates the active exertions of virtue from
the vague declamation of fenfibility.

K   The

The declaration of the National Aſſembly, when they recognized the rights of men, was calculated to touch the humane heart—the downfall of the clergy, to agitate the pupil of impulſe. On the watch to find fault, faults met your prying eye; a different prepoſſeſſion might have produced a different conviction.

When we read a book that ſupports our favourite opinions, how eagerly do we ſuck in the doctrines, and ſuffer our minds placidly to reflect the images that illuſtrate the tenets we have embraced. We indolently acquieſce in the concluſion, and our ſpirit animates and corrects the various ſubjects. But when, on the contrary, we peruſe a ſkilful writer, with whom we do not coincide in opinion, how attentive is the mind to detect fallacy. And this ſuſpicious coolneſs often prevents our being carried away by a ſtream of natural eloquence, which the prejudiced mind terms declamation—a pomp of words! We never allow

allow ourfelves to be warmed; and, after con-
tending with the writer, are more confirmed
in our opinion; as much, perhaps, from a
fpirit of contradiction as from reafon. A
lively imagination is ever in danger of being
betrayed into error by favourite opinions,
which it almoft perfonifies, the more effectually to intoxicate the underftanding. Always
tending to extremes, truth is left behind in
the heat of the chace, and things are viewed as
pofitively good, or bad, though they wear an
equivocal face.

Some celebrated writers have fuppofed that
wit and judgment were incompatible; oppofite
qualities, that, in a kind of elementary ftrife,
deftroyed each other: and many men of wit
have endeavoured to prove that they were
miftaken. Much may be adduced by wits
and metaphyficians on both fides of the queftion. But, from experience, I am apt to
believe that they do weaken each other, and

that

that great quicknefs of comprehenfion, and facile affociation of ideas, naturally preclude profundity of refearch. Wit is often a lucky hit; a moment of infpiration. We know not whence it comes, and it blows where it lifts. The operations of judgment, on the contrary, are cool and circumfpect; and coolnefs and deliberation are great enemies to enthufiafm. If wit is of fo fine a fpirit, that it almoft eva-porates when tranflated into another language, why may not the temperature have an influ-ence over it? This remark may be thought de-rogatory to the inferior qualities of the mind: but it is not a hafty one; and I mention it as a prelude to a conclufion I have frequently drawn, that the cultivation of reafon damps fancy. The bleffings of Heaven lie on each fide; we muft choofe, if we wifh to attain any degree of fuperiority, and not lofe our lives in laborious idlenefs. If we mean to build our knowledge or happinefs on a rational bafis,

we

we muſt learn to diſtinguiſh the poſſible, and not fight againſt the ſtream. And if we are careful to guard ourſelves from imaginary ſorrows and vain fears, we muſt alſo reſign many enchanting illuſions: for ſhallow muſt be the diſcernment which fails to diſcover that raptures and ecſtaſies ariſe from error.—Whether it will always be ſo, is not now to be diſcuſſed; ſuffice it to obſerve, that Truth is ſeldom arrayed by the Graces; and if ſhe charms, it is only by inſpiring a ſober ſatisfaction, which takes its riſe from a calm contemplation of proportion and ſimplicity. But, though it is allowed that one man has by nature more fancy than another, in each individual there is a ſpring-tide when fancy ſhould govern and amalgamate materials for the underſtanding; and a graver period, when theſe materials ſhould be employed by the judgment. For example, I am inclined to have a better opinion of the heart of an *old* man, who ſpeaks

K 3   of

of Sterne as his favourite author, than of his underſtanding. There are times and ſeaſons for all things: and moraliſts appear to me to err, when they would confound the gaiety of youth with the ſerioufneſs of age; for the virtues of age look not only more impoſing, but more natural, when they appear rather rigid. He who has not exerciſed his judgment to curb his imagination during the meridian of life, becomes, in its decline, too often the prey of childiſh feelings. Age demands reſpect; youth love : if this order is diſturbed, the emotions are not pure; and when love for a man in his grand climacteric takes place of reſpect; it, generally ſpeaking, borders on contempt. Judgment is ſublime, wit beautiful; and, according to your own theory, they cannot exiſt together without impairing each other's power. The predominancy of the latter, in your endleſs Reflections, ſhould lead haſty readers to ſuſpect that

3   it

it may, in a great degree, exclude the former.

But among all your plaufible arguments, and witty illuftrations, your contempt for the poor always appears confpicuous, and roufes my indignation. The following paragraph in particular ftruck me, as breathing the moft tyrannic fpirit, and difplaying the moft factitious feelings. ' Good order is the ' foundation of all good things. To be en-
' abled to acquire it, the people, without
' being fervile, muft be tractable and obe-
' dient. The magiftrate muft have his re-
' verence, the laws their authority. The
' body of the people muft not find the prin-
' ciples of natural fubordination by art rooted
' out of their minds. They *muft* refpect that
' property of which they *cannot* partake. *They*
' *muft labour to obtain what by labour can be*
' *obtained; and when they find, as they commonly*
' *do, the fuccefs difproportioned to the endeavour,*

K 4   ' they

' they muſt be taught their conſolation in the final
' proportions of eternal juſtice. Of this conſo-
' lation, whoever deprives them, deadens their
' induſtry, and ſtrikes at the root of all acqui-
' ſition as of all conſervation. He that does
' this, is the cruel oppreſſor, the mercileſs
' enemy, of the poor and wretched; at the
' ſame time that, by his wicked ſpeculations,
' he expoſes the fruits of ſucceſsful induſtry,
' and the accumulations of fortune, (ah! there's
the rub) ' to the plunder of the negligent, the
' diſappointed, and the unproſperous.'

This is contemptible hard-hearted ſophiſtry,
in the ſpecious form of humility, and ſub-
miſſion to the will of Heaven.—It is, Sir, *poſſible* to render the poor happier in this world,
without depriving them of the conſolation
which you gratuitouſly grant them in the
next. They have a right to more comfort
than they at preſent enjoy; and more comfort
might be afforded them, without encroaching

on

on the pleafures of the rich: not now waiting
to enquire whether the rich have any right to
exclufive pleafures. What do I fay?—encroaching! No; if an intercourfe were eftablifhed, it would impart the only true pleafure
that can be fnatched in this land of fhadows,
this hard fchool of moral difcipline.

I know, indeed, that there is often fomething difgufting in the diftreffes of poverty, at which the imagination revolts,
and ftarts back to exercife itfelf in the more
attractive Arcadia of fiction. The rich man
builds a houfe, art and tafte give it the higheft
finifh. His gardens are planted, and the trees
grow to recreate the fancy of the planter,
though the temperature of the climate may rather force him to avoid the dangerous damps
they exhale, than feek the umbrageous retreat.
Every thing on the eftate is cherifhed but
man;—yet, to contribute to the happinefs of
man, is the moft fublime of all enjoyments.

But

But if, inftead of fweeping pleafure-grounds, obelifks, temples, and elegant cottages, as *objeƐts* for the eye, the heart was allowed to beat true to nature, decent farms would be fcattered over the eftate, and plenty fmile around. Inftead of the poor being fubjeƐt to the griping hand of an avaricious fteward, they would be watched over with fatherly folicitude, by the man whofe duty and pleafure it was to guard their happinefs, and fhield from rapacity the beings who exalted him, by the fweat of their brow, above his fellows.

I could almoft imagine I fee a man thus gathering bleffings as he mounted the hill of life ; or confolation, in thofe days when the fpirits lag, and the tired heart finds no pleafure in them. It is not in fquandering alms that the poor can be relieved, or improved— it is the foftering fun of kindnefs, the wifdom that finds them employments calculated to give them habits of virtue, that meliorates their condition.

condition. Love is only the fruit of love; condefcenfion and authority may produce the obedience you applaud; but he has loft his heart of flefh who can fee a fellow-creature humbled before him, and trembling at the frown of a being, whofe heart is fupplied by the fame vital current, and whofe pride ought to be checked by a confcioufnefs of having the fame infirmities.

What falutary dews might not be fhed to refrefh this thirfty land, if men were more *enlightened!* Smiles and premiums might encourage cleanlinefs, induftry, and emulation. —A garden more inviting than Eden would then meet the eye, and fprings of joy murmur on every fide. The clergyman would fuperintend his own flock, the fhepherd would then love the fheep he daily tended; the fchool might rear its decent head, and the buzzing tribe, let loofe to play, impart a portion of their vivacious fpirits to the heart that longed

to

to open their minds, and lead them to taſte the pleaſures of men. Domeſtic pleaſure, the civilizing relations of huſband, brother, and father, would ſoften labour, and render life contented.

Returning once from a deſpotic country to a part of England well cultivated, but not very picturesque—with what delight did I not obſerve the poor man's garden!—The homely palings and twining woodbine, with all the ruſtic contrivances of ſimple, unlettered taſte, was a ſight which relieved the eye that had wandered indignant from the ſtately palace to the peſtiferous hovel, and turned from the awful contraſt into itſelf to mourn the fate of man, and curſe the arts of civilization!

Why cannot large eſtates be divided into ſmall farms? theſe dwellings would indeed grace our land. Why are huge foreſts ſtill allowed to ſtretch out with idle pomp and all the indolence of Eaſtern grandeur? Why do

the

the brown waftes meet the traveller's view, when men want work? But commons cannot be enclofed without *acts of parliament* to increafe the property of the rich ! Why might not the induftrious peafant be allowed to fteal a farm from the heath? This fight I have feen;—the cow that fupported the children grazed near the hut, and the cheerful poultry were fed by the chubby babes, who breathed a bracing air, far from the difeafes and the vices of cities. Domination blafts all thefe profpects; virtue can only flourifh amongft equals, and the man who fubmits to a fellow-creature, becaufe it promotes his worldly intereft, and he who relieves only becaufe it is his duty to lay up a treafure in heaven, are much on a par, for both are radically degraded by the habits of their life.

In this great city, that proudly rears its head, and boafts of its population and commerce, how much mifery lurks in peftilential

corners,

corners, whilft idle mendicants affail, on every
fide, the man who hates to encourage im-
poftors, or reprefs, with angry frown, the
plaints of the poor ! How many mechanics,
by a flux of trade or fafhion, lofe their em-
ployment; whom misfortunes, not to be ward-
ed off, lead to the idlenefs that vitiates their
chatacter and renders them afterwards averfe
to honeft labour ! Where is the eye that
marks thefe evils, more gigantic than any of
the infringements of property, which you
pioufly deprecate ? Are thefe remedilefs evils ?
And is the human heart fatisfied in turning
the poor over to *another* world, to receive the
bleffings this could afford ? If fociety was regulated on a more enlarged plan ; if man was
contented to be the friend of man, and did
not feek to bury the fympathies of humanity
in the fervile appellation of mafter ; if, turning
his eyes from ideal regions of tafte and elegance, he laboured to give the earth he in-
habited

habited all the beauty it is capable of receiving, and was ever on the watch to shed
abroad all the happiness which human nature
can enjoy;—he who, respecting the rights of
men, wishes to convince or persuade society
that this is true happiness and dignity, is not
the cruel *oppressor* of the poor, nor a short-
sighted philosopher—He fears God and loves
his fellow-creatures.—Behold the whole duty
of man !—the citizen who acts differently is
a sophisticated being.

Surveying civilized life, and feeing, with
undazzled eye, the polished vices of the rich,
their infincerity, want of natural affections, with
all the specious train that luxury introduces, I
have turned impatiently to the poor, to look
for man undebauched by riches or power—but,
alas ! what did I fee ? a being scarcely above
the brutes, over which it tyrannized; a broken
spirit, worn-out body, and all those gross vices
which the example of the rich, rudely copied,
could

could produce. Envy built a wall of feparation, that made the poor hate, whilft they bent to their fuperiors; who, on their part, ftepped afide to avoid the loathfome fight of human mifery.

What were the outrages of a day[k] to thefe continual miferies? Let thofe forrows hide their diminifhed head before the tremendous mountain of woe that thus defaces our globe! Man preys on man; and you mourn for the idle tapeftry that decorated a gothic pile, and the dronifh bell that fummoned the fat prieft to prayer. You mourn for the empty pageant of a name, when flavery flaps her wing, and the fick heart retires to die in lonely wilds, far from the abodes of man. Did the pangs you felt for infulted nobility, the anguifh that rent your heart when the gorgeous robes were torn off the idol human weaknefs had fet up, deferve to be compared with the long-drawn figh of melancholy re-

[k] The 6th of October.

flection,

flection, when mifery and vice thus feem to
haunt our fteps, and fwim on the top of every
cheering profpect? Why is our fancy to be
appalled by terrific perfpectives of a hell beyond the grave? — Hell ftalks abroad; — the
lafh refounds on the flave's naked fides; and
the fick wretch, who can no longer earn the
four bread of unremitting labour, fteals to a
ditch to bid the world a long good night—or,
neglected in fome oftentatious hofpital, breathes
its laft amidft the laugh of mercenary attend-
ants.

Such mifery demands more than tears —
I paufe to recollect myfelf; and fmother the
contempt I feel rifing for your rhetorical
flourifhes and infantine fenfibility.

Taking a retrofpective view of my hafty anfwer, and cafting a curfory glance over your
Reflections, I perceive that I have not alluded

L   to

to feveral reprehenfible paffages, in your ela-
borate work; which I marked for cenfure
when I firft perufed it with a fteady eye. And
now I find it almoft impoffible candidly to
refute your fophifms, without quoting your
own words, and putting the numerous contradictions I obferved in oppofition to each
other. This would be an effectual refutation;
but, after fuch a tedious drudgery, I fear I
fhould only be read by the patient eye that
fcarcely wanted my affiftance to detect the
flagrant errors. It would be a tedious procefs to
fhew, that often the moft juft and forcible
illuftrations are warped to colour over opinions *you* muft *fometimes* have fecretly defpifed;
or, at leaft, have difcovered, that what you
afferted without limitation, required the
greateft. Some fubjects of exaggeration may
have been fuperficially viewed : depth of
judgment is, perhaps, incompatible with the
predominant features of your mind. Your

reafon

reason may have often been the dupe of
your imagination; but fay, did you not fometimes angrily bid her be ftill, when fhe whif-
pered that you were departing from ftrict
truth? Or, when affuming the awful form of
confcience, and only fmiling at the vagaries of
vanity, did fhe not aufterely bid you recollect
your own errors, before you lifted the aveng-
ing ftone? Did fhe not fometimes wave her
hand, when you poured forth a torrent of
fhining fentences, and befeech you to con-
catenate them—plainly telling you that the
impaffioned eloquence of the heart was calculated rather to affect than dazzle the reader,
whom it hurried along to conviction? Did fhe
not anticipate the remark of the wife, who drink
not at a fhallow fparkling ftream, and tell you
that they would difcover when, with the dignity of fincerity, you fupported an opinion that
only appeared to you with one face; or, when

fuperannuated

superannuated vanity made you ranfack your invention ?—But I forbear.

I have before animadverted on our method of electing reprefentatives, convinced that it debauches both the morals of the people and the candidates, without rendering the member really refponfible, or attached to his conftituents; but, amongft your other contradictions, you blame the National Affembly for expecting any exertions from the fervile principle of refponfibility, and afterwards infult them for not rendering themfelves refponfible. Whether the one the French have adopted will anfwer the purpofe better, and be more than a fhadow of reprefentation, time only can fhew. In theory it appears more promifing.

Your real or artificial affection for the Englifh conftitution feems to me to refemble the brutal affection of fome weak characters. They think it a duty to love their relations

3   with

with a blind, indolent tendernefs, that *will not*
fee the faults it might affift to correct, if their
affection had been built on rational grounds.
They love they know not why, and they will
love to the end of the chapter.

Is it abfolute blafphemy to doubt of the omnipotence of the law, and to fuppofe that religion might be more pure if there were fewer
baits for hypocrites in the church? But our
manners, you tell us, are drawn from the
French, though you had before celebrated our
native plainnefs. If they were, it is time we
broke loofe from dependance——Time that
Englifhmen drew water from their own
fprings; for, if manners are not a painted
fubftitute for morals, we have only to cultivate our reafon, and we fhall not feel the
want of an arbitrary model. Nature will fuf-
fice; but I forget myfelf:—Nature and Reafon, according to your fyftem, are all to give

place

place to authority; and the gods, as Shakefpeare makes a frantic wretch exclaim, feem
to kill us for their fport, as men do flies.

THE END.

For EU product safety concerns, contact us at Calle de José Abascal, 56–1°, 28003 Madrid, Spain or eugpsr@cambridge.org.

www.ingramcontent.com/pod-product-compliance
Ingram Content Group UK Ltd.
Pitfield, Milton Keynes, MK11 3LW, UK
UKHW012340130625
459647UK00009B/418